What Church Leaders Say about Alpha

"Out of England comes an exciting new program which is moving churches around the world from maintenance to mission. Alpha is a well-designed, implementable program that addresses the basic questions of life for the churched and unchurched alike. Through Alpha, Jesus Christ is capturing the hearts and minds of an ever-growing number of persons. The course meets the vital test of being both open and faithful—welcoming of all, while presenting the gospel message with clarity and power."

George Gallup, Jr.
Chairman, The George H. Gallup International Institute

"The Alpha Course is a most engaging way of passing on the basics of Christianity. It is a tool for evangelism and nurture that I highly recommend."

J. I. Packer
Professor of Theology, Regent College, Vancouver, Canada

"Alpha seems especially blessed in that the Lord is using it to reach all sorts of people in all sorts of spiritual conditions. Genius is the art of taking the complex and communicating it with warmth and simplicity. If you've ever wondered 'Why Jesus?' you'll hardly find a better answer than this."

Luis Palau
Evangelist

"I know of many people whose lives have been transformed through the Alpha Course. I rejoice at how God is using it so powerfully to renew many churches both inside and outside prison walls."

Charles W. Colson
Prison Fellowship Ministries

"We stand alongside others who have a similar passion for leading people into relationships with Jesus Christ. We applaud the vision and work of Alpha to connect the unconnected to the life of the local church and to relationship with Jesus Christ."

Bill Hybels
Senior Pastor, Willow Creek Community Church
Chairman of the Board, Willow Creek Association

"I have met many unlikely people from different backgrounds who have been profoundly changed through attending this course."

Jackie Pullinger
Hong Kong

HOW TO RUN THE ALPHA COURSE

THE DIRECTOR'S HANDBOOK

Alpha

For Alpha Directors, Leaders, and Helpers

By the same author:
Why Jesus?
Why Christmas?
Questions of Life
Searching Issues
A Life Worth Living
Challenging Lifestyle
How to Run the Alpha Course: Telling Others
30 Days
The Heart of Revival

How to Run the Alpha Course: The Director's Handbook, revised edition
Portions of this handbook are taken from *How to Run the Alpha Course: Telling Others* by Nicky Gumbel.

Revised edition first published 2001 by Alpha North America, 74 Trinity Place, New York, NY 10006

Cover and interior illustrations by Charlie Mackesy

ISBN 1-931808-287

2 3 4 5 6 7 8 9 10 Printing/Year 06 05 04 03

Table of Contents

How to Use This Book

The purpose of this book is to provide you with the information necessary to run a high quality Alpha Course, including what it is it, how to set up and run a course, as well as the principles behind Alpha. It will also put into your hands easy-to-use resources and reproducible forms. If you are an Alpha Course Director (or Administrator)—the person responsible for all details related to setting up and running an effective Alpha Course—this book is for you.

We also recommend that you obtain a copy of *How to Run the Alpha Course: Telling Others* (referred to in this book simply as *Telling Others*), a book which goes into extensive detail about the philosophy and practicalities of running the Alpha Course. It is helpful for Small-Group Leaders and Helpers to have a copy of *Telling Others* so they can see how they fit into the big picture and understand the philosophy of Alpha. Since Alpha is an ongoing evangelism ministry, it is important that it has the support of the entire church. Your church's entire staff and leadership team would also benefit from reading *Telling Others*.

There are three parts to this book.

Part I gives the history, theology, and vision behind Alpha. In this section (pages 11-21) you will:
- Read the history and background of Alpha.
- Learn how God is using Alpha worldwide to bring renewal and new life to people of all backgrounds.
- Master the basic terminology.
- Gain an understanding of the biblical foundation of the course.
    This portion of the book is helpful to read during the decision process concerning an Alpha Course. It is essential that everyone on the Alpha Team is exposed to the content of at least chapters 1 and 2.

Part II includes more of the nuts and bolts of setting up and running an Alpha Course:
- It includes "how tos" and tips for success based on ministry at Holy Trinity Brompton Church (HTB) in London.
- The church's leadership will want to master this material in order to effectively communicate with others in the church and to train the Small-Group Leaders and Helpers and other members of the Alpha Team.
- The Alpha Director will need a copy to gain an understanding of the practical aspects of the course.
- The small group leaders and helpers will also benefit by having a copy to refer to throughout their training and during the course itself, although this is not essential.

Part III includes dozens of reproducible resources to assist in the setting up and running of an Alpha Course. Among the helpful tools are:

- a detailed planning timeline,
- job descriptions for all Alpha Team positions,
- a complete listing of Alpha resources and related suggested reading,
- schedules for evening and daytime Alpha courses and the weekend away,
- a sample press release and bulletin insert to help promote your local course,
- an Alpha Questionnaire,
- other miscellaneous forms, as well as the Alpha copyright statement.

Why is high-quality administration important on Alpha? There are two main reasons. The first involves image; non-churchgoers often expect church to be inefficiently organized and half-hearted in its approach. However, if your administration is well done, your guests may be pleasantly surprised and their preconceptions may be broken. This could make it easier for them to hear the Gospel message.

The second reason to emphasize administration is that it promotes Christian friendship. By taking the time and trouble to create effective administration, we can show some kind of care and attention to each individual. For example, for a guest, having a name badge waiting upon arrival at an Alpha Course could make all the difference in his or her perceived involvement in the course. As we express our commitment to them, the guests tend to feel more committed to the course.

There is a lot of work involved in administrating an Alpha Course. However, it is spread over time and there are many resources available which will help you. Delegate as much as you can and build a team around you. Surround each step with prayer. Thousands of churches all over the world have run Alpha courses successfully, following the model laid out in this handbook. We would encourage you to do the very best you can with the human and finanical resources you have available, to follow the guidelines presented here.

Part I

An Overview of

The Alpha Course

Alpha

1
History

by Nicky Gumbel

Thousands of people around the world are now taking part in the Alpha Course—a ten-week practical introduction to the Christian faith designed primarily for nonchurchgoers and those who have recently become Christians. In May 1993 we hosted a conference at Holy Trinity Brompton Anglican Church in England (HTB) for church leaders who wanted to run such courses. Over a thousand people came, and hundreds of Alpha courses began all over the UK as a result. Since then, Alpha courses have been introduced in the U.S. and Canada, and to over 120 countries worldwide. The number of Alpha courses in operation is growing daily.

Alpha has evolved from what was essentially a basic introduction for new Christians to something which is aimed primarily at those outside the church. Alpha began as a home group in 1976 in the living room of Charles Marnham, a clergyman at HTB. Charles had a desire to reach others around him with the simple truths of the Christian faith. He began looking for a means of presenting the basic principles of the Christian faith to new Christians in a relaxed and informal setting. With this goal in mind, he devised the concept of the Alpha Course.

A few people gathered together in his living room each Wednesday evening for a light meal, a talk, and discussion groups. When Charles moved on, John Irvine took it over in 1981. He lengthened the course to ten weeks and added a weekend for teaching on the person and work of the Holy Spirit. When Nicky Lee took it over in 1985, there were about thirty-five people attending each of three annual courses and under his leadership that grew to well over a hundred. By the time I took over the Alpha Course in the early 1990s, Alpha was central to the church's life. Since then it has grown again to 1,000 people (including the leadership team) on each course (three a year).

During my second Alpha Course I made a discovery which transformed the church's approach to the course and later brought Alpha to the attention of churches throughout the UK and internationally. As I looked around at the 13 members of my small group, I was surprised that besides the three Christian helpers, all other members were nonchurchgoers.

It was astonishing. This group raised all the normal objections: "What about other religions?" "What about suffering?" and so on. We had a stormy first six weeks, but the entire group went on the weekend away.

At the weekend away, which focuses on the person and work of the Holy Spirit, all 10 announced their Christian conversion. When we came back from the weekend away, we had the most amazing evening listening to all their testimonies.

This experience transformed my thinking about Alpha. I realized how this simple course in basic Christianity could become a powerful tool for evangelism.

Adjustments were made in the method of welcome, the atmosphere of the small groups, the food, the seating, the flowers, the sound, and the content of the actual talks. We emphasized that everyone should be allowed to ask any question they liked in their small groups. Nothing should be treated as too trivial, threatening, or illogical. Every question would be addressed courteously and thoughtfully. It also became a policy that the people were given the freedom to return or not. No one was going to pursue them. The course grew quickly—so quickly that the location had to be changed and the Alpha Team of helpers massively increased.

GROWTH OF ALPHA

The course has been steadily growing since my second course. The growth comes through "Friends bringing friends." At the end of each course at HTB there is a Celebration Dinner which now attracts around 1,000 people. This is one of the key events for bringing people to the next course. People who are converted on Alpha have a circle of people to bring to the dinner and invite on the next course. People often bring their family and friends to the next Alpha, and that is how it grows.

One young man came and then he brought his parents, who are now leaders on the course. Then he brought his girlfriend, who also became a Christian. It's all friendship-based. There's no knocking on doors. There's little advertising. It's simply "Friends bringing friends."

This same model is now being used effectively in over 17,000 courses in 121 countries worldwide. An estimated 425,000 people are involved with an Alpha Course somewhere in the world each week. This includes the Alpha Team (those who host and run Alpha) and the guests who are searching for answers to the questions of life. Almost every type of Christian church, including, but not limited to, Anglican, Assemblies of God, Baptist, Christian Missionary Alliance, Congregational, Episcopal, Lutheran, Methodist, Pentecostal, Presbyterian, Roman Catholic, United Church of Christ, and Vineyard Fellowship is running Alpha. Independent and non-denominational churches also hold Alpha courses.

The growth of Alpha worldwide has been very encouraging. Attendance has grown from a total of about 500 people in four courses during 1991 to an estimated attendance of more than 2.5 million in 2000. Over 15,000 churches worldwide participate in this program, including more than 2,000 churches in the United States. Courses are now running in about 50 countries in addition to England, Canada, and the United States. The table below shows estimated attendance at Alpha Courses from 1991–2000.

Year	People
1991	500
1992	1,000
1993	4,500
1994	30,000
1995	100,000
1996	250,000
1997	300,000
1998	435,000
1999	1,500,000
2000	2,500,000

ALPHA IN NORTH AMERICA

Throughout North America lives are being touched by God's love through the ministry of the Holy Spirit. Churches that host an Alpha Course or an Alpha Conference are encouraged as they see the impact on their congregations and communities.

Following an Alpha Conference in Toronto, Ted Ward, chair of the evangelism group of the host church, said, "With 700 delegates, 90 volunteers, 150 churches, and 25 denominations represented, we see this as the largest conference on evangelism ever held by Canadian Anglicans. The most encouraging thing is that it is God at work. It has to be, otherwise you wouldn't see this kind of snowballing effect."[1]

According to Justin Dennison, senior pastor of South Hills Community Church in California, Alpha has "made a bridge between those on the fringe of faith with those who are deeply involved. [I'm] amazed at the people who come and the friends they invite. Nothing has impacted our church at a greater level than this."[2]

Elaine Young, wife of the rector of Bridgetown, Nova Scotia, wrote the following: "The spiritual impact of Alpha upon our community has been significant. We expect that it will prove to be an integral part of the renewal that God has begun in our parish. But the success of this program lies not in itself. By revealing the reality of the power of Jesus Christ to forgive, to release, empower, and equip, new life begins for so many who are in need of God."[3]

Susan Baker-Borjeson, rector at St. Peter's Episcopal Church in South Dartmouth, Mass., states: "Alpha has been God's answer to one of my dearest prayers....We are networking with other churches in our area about Alpha, encouraging them to run the course....Three and a half years into Alpha, we are not just alive in Christ, we are reverberating for Christ!"[4]

RESOURCES FOR GETTING STARTED

As Alpha has grown throughout the UK and now internationally, it seemed sensible to pass on some of the things we have learned over the years. Therefore we have developed Alpha Conferences and a variety of print, video, and audio resources. Historically we have found the easiest way to learn how to "do Alpha" is to hear from others who are running effective courses. There are two major areas of Alpha: setting up the course and running the course.

SETTING UP THE ALPHA COURSE

The first way to learn about how to get Alpha started is to attend an Alpha Conference. Regional training sessions are held on the principles, philosophy, and practicalities of the Alpha Course. Churches have found it helpful to send their leadership teams to these conferences to capture the vision of Alpha and to gain an understanding of the basic "how tos." (See page 37 for more information on Alpha Conferences.)

There are also a number of helpful resources that can be used to share the vision of Alpha with others in the church and to train the Alpha Team. These resources include:

Title	Description
• *The Alpha Course Introductory Video*	Fifteen-minute overview of Alpha
• *Telling Others*	The vision, the excitement, the challenge of Alpha

- *How to Run Alpha Video*   Two video sessions on the Principles and Practicalities of Alpha

- The *Alpha Leader's Training DVD* or *Video*   Three training sessions on Leading Small Groups, Pastoral Care, and Ministry

- *The Alpha Course Leader's Guide*   Part I is used to train the Small-Group Leaders and Helpers

RUNNING THE ALPHA COURSE

A variety of materials have been developed to assist local churches and individuals in implementing an Alpha Course. Following are a listing and brief description of each resource.

Title	Description
• Invitation Brochures	4-color, ready to customize (packs of 50)
• *Questions of Life*	The Alpha Course in book form
• *The Alpha Course DVDs* or *Videos*	5-video or 2 DVD set including 15 talks
• *Why Jesus?* or *Why Christmas?*	Presentation of the Gospel
• *The Alpha Course Manual*	Talk outlines and room for notetaking for each participant and for Small-Group Leader and Helper
• *The Alpha Course Leader's Guide*	Part II includes suggestions for group discussions and Bible studies for Small-Group Leaders and Helpers
• *Searching Issues*	Biblical help with key objections to Christianity

The table on page 95 shows how these resources correlate with each other.

NOTES

1. As quoted in *Alpha News*, "In Brief," November 1996, p.33.
2. As quoted in *Alpha News*, "The International Scene," November 1996, p. 26. Reprinted with permission from Holy Trinity Brmpton, London. Originally quoted in *Christian Week*, a Canadian newspaper.
3. As quoted in *Alpha News*, "In Brief," November 1996, p. 33. Reprinted with permission from Holy Trinity Brompton, London. Originally printed in *The Prayer Book Society of Canada Newsletter* in July 1996.
4. As quoted in *Alpha News*, December 2000-March 2001 issue., page 8. Reprinted with permission from Holy Trinity Brompton, London.

2
Principles

by Nicky Gumbel

When I came to you, brothers, I did not come with eloquence or superior wisdom as I proclaimed to you the testimony about God. For I resolved to know nothing while I was with you except Jesus Christ and him crucified. I came to you in weakness and fear, and with much trembling. My message and my preaching were not with wise and persuasive words, but with a demonstration of the Spirit's power, so that your faith might not rest on men's wisdom, but on God's power. —1 Corinthians 2:1-5

I am not a natural evangelist. I have never found it easy to talk to my friends about Jesus Christ. Some people are completely natural evangelists: they find it the easiest thing in the world.

When I first became a Christian, I was so excited about what had happened that I longed for everybody to follow suit. After I had been a Christian for only a few days I went to a party, determined to tell everyone. I saw a friend dancing and decided the first step was to make her realize her need for Jesus. So I went up to her and said, "You look awful. You really need Jesus." She thought I had gone mad. It was not the most effective way of telling someone the Good News. (However, she did later become a Christian, quite independently of me, and she is now my wife!)

If we charge around like a bull in a china shop, sooner or later we get hurt. Even if we approach the subject sensitively, we may still get hurt. When we do, we tend to withdraw. Certainly this was my experience. After a few years, I moved from the danger of insensitivity and fell into the opposite danger of fear.

There was a time (ironically, when I was in seminary) when I became fearful of even talking about Jesus to those who were not Christians. Ever since then I've been looking for ways in which ordinary people like me, who aren't naturally gifted evangelists, can communicate their faith with friends, family, and colleagues without feeling fearful or risking insensitivity. I was excited to discover that Alpha is evangelism for ordinary people. All of us involved with Alpha have sensed the extraordinary blessing of God upon it.

When Alpha first started growing, I thought, "How could something that started in Central London work elsewhere?" Alpha currently runs in dozens of countries, including Zimbabwe, Kenya, Norway, Denmark, Sweden, Germany, Malaysia, Hong Kong, Australia, New Zealand, United States, Canada, and many more.

Why does Alpha, which started in London, operate so effectively in different countries and cultures? I believe it is because the Alpha Course is based on six New Testament principles. In this chapter, I want to look at each of these principles in turn.

PRINCIPLE 1: EVANGELISM[1] IS MOST EFFECTIVE THROUGH THE LOCAL CHURCH

John Stott, author of many books and Rector Emeritus of All Souls, Langham Place in England, has described evangelism through the local church as "the most normal, natural and productive method of spreading the Gospel today."[2] Of course, other forms of evangelism work too. Missions and Billy Graham-style crusades clearly have been greatly used by God. They raise the profile of the church and are still effective means of bringing people to Christ. But missions are more likely to bear lasting fruit if they are based in an ongoing program of local church evangelism, which has the great advantage of continuity of relationships.

WHAT YOU SEE IS WHAT YOU GET

Someone may respond at a crusade or mission and be referred to their local church. They may be disappointed to find the environment of the church radically different from the meeting which attracted them in the first place and so they subsequently stop attending. This is one of the reasons that follow-up after big crusades is so hard. By contrast, if someone is introduced to Christianity at their local church, they become familiar with the place and the people, and are therefore much more likely to stay.

MOBILIZES A WHOLE ARMY OF EVANGELISTS

Evangelism through the local church involves not just one great evangelist, or even an evangelist in a team, but a whole army of evangelists. On every one of our Alpha courses at Holy Trinity Brompton in London, we have at least 120 people involved in evangelism. Throughout a whole year perhaps 250 different people are involved. This is excellent training for these people and taps into a resource which might otherwise have remained dormant in the church.

A recent Gallup survey in the USA claimed that only 10 percent of church members are active in any form of personal ministry, but that 40 percent have expressed an interest. Alpha is one way of mobilizing these people. Reports coming back from churches time and again speak of the effect Alpha has had on their church. People are excited to see new people coming to Christ, to welcome them into their congregation, and to see their own part in this process.

FRIENDSHIP-BASED

If someone comes to Christ on the course and is filled with the Spirit, they will naturally tell their friends, family, and colleagues. They will say to them, "Come and see! Come to the next course!" Then many more people come to the next course and they all have circles of friends which get penetrated. This is a New Testament model of evangelism: Peter brought his brother Andrew; Philip brought his friend Nathaniel; the woman at the well went back and told everyone in her town; and Matthew the tax collector threw a party and invited all his work colleagues to meet Jesus. This is the way Alpha works.

THE MORE CHECKOUTS, THE MORE CUSTOMERS

This is a principle of the supermarket that we learned from the Americans. The more churches running Alpha or another evangelism program, the more people who will be reached by Christ. Suppose that out of the 300,000+ churches in America and the 28,000 in Canada every one was running an effective program of evangelism week in and week out, month in and month out, and year in and year out. Imagine how quickly the continent could be reached for Christ.

PRINCIPLE 2: EVANGELISM IS A PROCESS

NEW TESTAMENT EXPRESSIONS

Conversion may take place in a moment but it is part of a process. All New Testament expressions of conversion are process words. Jesus used the expression "born again" (John 3:3) for the beginning of a spiritual life, and the New Testament speaks about becoming a child of God. While the birth of a child may be a onetime event, there is a much longer process before and afterward.

Alpha is a ten-week course involving a total of 15 talks which include a weekend away and a Celebration Dinner at the end. We do not expect people to respond to the Gospel after the first week (although some do). We recognize that people need time to think, watch, listen, and talk through their questions and difficulties. Each person is beginning at a different stage.

Some are already Christians but will often say, in retrospect, that at the start of the course they were Christians "without any real experience of God." Others are at the point of new birth when they begin Alpha. Many are still a long way off when they begin Alpha. Some are convinced atheists, some are New Agers, some are adherents to other religions or cults. Many are living in lifestyles which are far from Christian. We welcome everyone. Some will complete the whole course and still not be Christians at the end; we hope they will be unable to say they have not heard the Gospel. Others will give their lives to Christ somewhere on the course. For nearly all of them, Alpha will enable them to take a step forward in their relationship with God.

PROCESS OPERATES AT TWO LEVELS

Gradually seeing the picture

First is the level of understanding. The fact there is a process of evangelism spread over 15 sessions enables us to give more attention to aspects of the Christian faith than one would be able to in one evangelistic talk. For example, in 1994 I saw a man named Guy standing at the back of the room who looked very uncomfortable and worried. When I introduced myself, he said, "I don't want to be here, I've been dragged along." I said, "Great! Let me introduce you to 11 other people who don't want to be here," and I took him to meet my small group. At the end of the evening I heard Guy talking to someone else in the group. "Are you coming back next week?" he asked. The other man replied, "Yes, I'll be here." To which Guy said, "Well, if you're coming back next week, I'll come back next week." Six weeks later he said to me, "This course is like a jigsaw puzzle. Every time I come back another piece fits into place. And I'm beginning to get the picture."

Building trust

Furthermore, the fact that Alpha is a process enables trust to develop. This is the second level. There is a great deal of cynicism, skepticism, and distrust about the Christian church. Many people wonder if the church is after their money, their mind, or something else. It can take a few weeks for a level of trust to build. As the guests get to know their Small-Group Leaders, they begin to see that the Alpha Team is not "after" anything and they start to listen.

PRINCIPLE 3: EVANGELISM INVOLVES THE WHOLE PERSON

Evangelism involves an appeal to the whole person. Pope John Paul II, speaking to bishops from Japan, said that "evangelization. . . must touch people's minds and hearts, stir their consciences, and engage all their energies." Indeed, each talk on Alpha is designed to appeal to the mind, heart, conscience and will, although in some of the talks the emphasis will be on just one of those aspects.

APPEAL TO THE MIND

We appeal to the mind because we believe that Christianity is based in history: on the life, death, and resurrection of Jesus Christ. We preach "Jesus Christ and him crucified" (1 Cor. 2:2). We seek to persuade with every argument we can muster, just as Paul did on so many occasions (for example, Acts 18:4). We try to teach only what we can establish from the Bible and we point people to the biblical text. We do not expect anyone to take a "blind leap" of faith. Rather, we hope they will take a reasonable step of faith based on reasonable grounds.

APPEAL TO THE HEART AND THE CONSCIENCE

Secondly, we appeal to the heart. Our message does not simply require an assent of the intellect to a series of propositions, rather it calls people to a love-relationship with Jesus Christ. John Stott has written:

> There is a place for emotion in spiritual experience. The Holy Spirit's . . . ministry is not limited to illuminating our minds and teaching us about Christ. He also pours God's love into our hearts. Similarly, he bears witness with our spirit that we are God's children, for he causes us to say "Abba, Father" and to exclaim with gratitude, "How great is the love the Father has lavished on us, that we should be called children of God!"[3]

The Gospel involves both the rational and the experiential and it impacts both those from an Enlightenment background who need to experience God and those who have sought experiences but who need to understand the truth about God.

Thirdly, we seek to appeal to the conscience. Paul writes, "By setting forth the truth plainly we commend ourselves to everyone's conscience in the sight of God" (2 Cor 4:2). We know that every person has a conscience. Deep down we all have a sense of right and wrong. The Holy Spirit, often working through people's consciences, convinces tham about sin. Their consciences therefore are on our side. Throughout the course we are appealing to this side in urging people to repent and turn to Christ.

APPEAL TO THE WILL

Fourthly, we seek to appeal to the will. We recognize, of course, that no one can come to the Father unless God calls them. As Jesus said, "No one knows the Son except the Father, and no one knows the Father except the Son and those to whom the Son chooses to reveal him" (Matt. 11:27). On the other hand, Jesus went on to say in the very next verse, "Come to me, all you who are weary and burdened, and I will give you rest" (vs. 28). In other words, He called for a decision.

There is a difference between an appeal to the will and the wrong form of pressure. We try to avoid all forms of pressure on Alpha. We do not endlessly exhort anyone to respond or chase after people if they do not come back: it is up to them to decide. Over the period of 10 weeks, as we pray and allow the Holy Spirit to do His work, giving people the opportunity to respond, we are, in effect, making a continuous appeal to their wills.

PRINCIPLE 4:
MODELS OF EVANGELISM IN THE NEW TESTAMENT INCLUDE CLASSICAL, HOLISTIC, AND POWER EVANGELISM

Graham Tomlin, lecturer at Wycliffe Hall Theological College, Oxford, draws attention to three different models of evangelism.[4] Clearly these three are not mutually exclusive and we very much hope that the Alpha Course involves all three models.

CLASSICAL EVANGELISM (WORDS)

Classical evangelism involves "the proclamation of the unchanging message." Certainly, at the heart of Alpha is the proclamation of the Gospel of Jesus Christ: the first talk is about Christ's deity, the second is about His death on the cross for us, and each talk has at its core some principle of Christian belief and living.

HOLISTIC EVANGELISM (WORKS)

Evangelism and social action go hand in hand. The latter involves both social justice in the removal of injustice, inhumanity, and inequality, and social service in relieving human need, such as hunger, homelessness, and poverty. We attempt during Alpha to avoid the dangers of pietism or super spiritualism by our teaching and example, believing that evangelism is fundamentally linked to social responsibility.

POWER EVANGELISM (WONDERS)

Third, there is power evangelism, where the proclamation of the Gospel goes hand in hand with a demonstration of the Spirit's power (for example, 1 Corinthians 2:1-5). We include this third element because we believe it is firmly based in New Testament practice.

The coming of the Kingdom of God involved not only the spoken proclamation of the Gospel but also a visible demonstration of its presence by signs, wonders, and miracles. Each of the Gospel writers expected these to continue.

In the Book of Acts this continues beyond the time Jesus was on earth. After the outpouring of the Holy Spirit, there is a remarkable continuation of supernatural power, ranging from speaking in tongues to raising the dead. These demonstrations of power continue right through to the last chapter (Acts 28:7-9). Throughout Acts we see the outworking of this commission. The disciples continued to preach and teach, but also to heal the sick, raise the dead, and cast out demons (Acts 3:1-10; 4:12; 5:12-16; 8:5-13; 9:32-43; 14:3, 8-10; 19:11-12; 20:9-12; 28:8-9).

Signs and miracles were a central part of Paul's proclamation of the Gospel (Rom. 15:19). It is also clear from 1 Corinthians 12-14 that Paul did not believe that such abilities were confined to the apostles and he expected the more obviously supernatural gifts of the Spirit to continue in an effective and healthy church. He speaks about "gifts of healing," "miraculous powers," "prophecy," "speaking in different kinds of tongues," and "the interpretation of tongues." He described these as being given to different members of the Body of Christ and as being the work of the Spirit (1 Cor. 12:7-11).

Likewise, the writer to the Hebrews says that God testified to His message by "signs, wonders and various miracles, and gifts of the Holy Spirit" (Heb 2:4). Nowhere in the Bible is the supernatural display of the power of the Holy Spirit confined to any particular period of history. On the contrary, such signs, wonders, and miracles are part of the Kingdom which was inaugurated by Jesus Christ and continues to this day. Hence we should expect today to see the supernatural display of the power of the Holy Spirit as part of His kingdom activity and as an authentication of the Good News. However, we do not draw ultimate attention to the signs and wonders, but to the God of love who performs them.

PRINCIPLE 5:
EVANGELISM IN THE POWER OF THE HOLY SPIRIT IS BOTH DYNAMIC AND EFFECTIVE

On the Day of Pentecost Peter preached with such power that the people were "cut to the heart" and 3000 were converted (Acts 2:37-41). The remarkable events continued: "Everyone was filled with awe, and many wonders and miraculous signs were done by the apostles. . . . And the Lord added to their number daily those who were being saved" (vss. 43-47).

Remarkable healings followed (e.g., Acts 3:1-10). People were astonished and came running to find out what had happened (vs. 11). Peter and John preached the Gospel with great boldness: "When they saw the courage of Peter and John and realized that they were unschooled, ordinary men, they were astonished and they took note that these men had been with Jesus. But since they could see the man who had been healed standing there with them, there was nothing they could say" (Acts 4:13-14).

People continued to be converted. "So the word of God spread. The number of disciples in Jerusalem increased rapidly, and a large number of priests became obedient to the faith" (Acts 6:7). As we go on in the Book of Acts the same pattern continues.

Luke tells us what happened to 12 Ephesian men: "When Paul placed his hands on them, the Holy Spirit came on them, and they spoke in tongues and prophesied" (Acts 19:6). Further, in Ephesus, "God did extraordinary miracles through Paul, so that even handkerchiefs and aprons that had touched him were taken to the sick, and their illnesses were cured and the evil spirits left them" (vss. 11-12).

Far from dwindling away through the period covered by the Book of Acts, this spiritual dynamic continued. Even in the last chapter we read of Paul praying for Publius's father: "His father was sick in bed, suffering from fever and dysentery. Paul went in to see him and, after prayer, placed his hands on him and healed him. When this had happened, the rest of the sick on the island came and were cured" (Acts 28:8-9). All the way through Acts we see the dynamic effect of the coming of the kingdom of God accompanied by conversions, miraculous signs, healings, visions, tongues, prophecy, raising the dead, and casting out evil spirits.

The same God is at work today among us. Evangelism can still be dynamic and effective. We are finding this to be the case on the Alpha Course, not only at HTB but all over the country and in different parts of the world.

PRINCIPLE 6:
EFFECTIVE EVANGELISM REQUIRES THE FILLING AND REFILLING OF THE SPIRIT

Jesus told His disciples, "You will receive power when the Holy Spirit comes on you; and you will be my witnesses in Jerusalem, and in all Judea and Samaria, and to the ends of the earth" (Acts 1:8). On the Day of Pentecost the promise of Jesus was fulfilled and "all of them were filled with the Holy Spirit and began to speak in other tongues as the Spirit enabled them" (Acts 2:4).

However, it did not end there. Later on we read of Peter being "filled with the Holy Spirit" again (Acts 4:8). Still later the disciples (including Peter) were filled again (Acts 4:31). The filling of the Holy Spirit is not a onetime experience. Paul urges the Christians of Ephesus to "be filled with the Spirit" (Eph 5:18) and the emphasis is on continuing to be filled.

Professor Wayne Grudem writes the most useful chapter I know of on this subject in his masterful *Systematic Theology*.[5] Sometimes people use the analogy of a glass of water for people being filled with the Spirit. Either the glass is empty or full. Dr. Grudem points out that people are not like that. He says a better analogy would be a balloon because it can be full of air but then it can be more and more full. Like all analogies this one breaks down if you take it too far. The point he makes is that we all need more of the Holy Spirit, and Jesus is the only person who has the Holy Spirit without measure.

I think that there can be little doubt that the greatest evangelist of our century has been Billy Graham (born 1918). In an authorized biography John Pollock tells how Billy Graham visited Hildenborough Hall in 1947 and heard Stephen Olford speak on the subject "Be not drunk—but be filled with the Spirit." Billy Graham asked to see Olford privately and Olford expounded the fullness of the Holy Spirit in the life of a believer. "At the close of the second day they prayed 'like Jacob of old laying hold of God,'" recalls Olford, "crying, 'Lord, I will not let Thee go except Thou bless me,' until we came to a place of rest and praising"; and Graham said, "I'm filled. This is a turning point in my life. This will revolutionize my ministry."[6]

One of the keys to Alpha is having a team of Spirit-filled people using every gift they possess to lead others to Christ. Those who come to Christ on the course know that a radical change has occurred in their lives because they have been filled with the Holy Spirit. This experience of God gives them the stimulus and power to invite their friends to the next Alpha.

Notes

1. Leading missiologist David Bosch defines evangelism as the proclamation of salvation in Christ to those who do not believe in Him, calling them to repentance and conversion, announcing forgiveness of sin, inviting them to become living members of Christ's earthly community and to begin a life of service to others in the power of the Holy Spirit.

2. John Stott, *The Contemporary Christian* (Nottingham, England: IVP, 1992), p. 241.

3. John Stott, *The Contemporary Christian* (Nottingham, England: InterVarsity Press, 1992), pp. 121, 127.

4. Graham Tomlin, *Evangelical Anglicans*, edited by R. T. France and A. E. McGrath (London:SPCK, 1993), pp. 82-95.

5. Wayne Grudem, *Systematic Theology* (Nottingham, England: IVP, 1994), pp. 763-787.

6. John Pollock, *Billy Graham* (London, England: Hodder & Stoughton, 1966), pp. 62-63.

Part II

Setting Up and Running

The Alpha Course

Alpha

3
Practicalities

Whatever you do, work at it with all your heart, as working for the Lord, not for men, since you know that you will receive an inheritance from the Lord as a reward. —Colossians 3:23-24

UNDERSTANDING ALPHA

To those attending as guests, Alpha is a practical introduction to the Christian faith. To those running the course (The Church Leader, Alpha Director, Small Group Leaders and Helpers, Worship Team, and Task Force Members), it is friendship-based evangelism.

The following acronym helps explain what Alpha is and sums up some of the key ingredients of Alpha:

Anyone can come. Anyone interested in finding out more about the Christian faith can be invited on this ten-week introduction designed for nonchurch-goers and new Christians. It can also be used as a refresher course for mature Christians. In many churches the first course is attended mainly by church members and later fringe members and then the unchurched.

Learning and laughter. The course is based on a series of fifteen talks which tackle the key questions at the heart of the Christian faith. (These talks can be given by a leader or there are tapes or videos available depending on group size.) It is possible to learn about the Christian faith and to enjoy the experience! Laughter and fun are a key part of the course, breaking down barriers and enabling everyone to relax together.

Pasta. An opportunity to eat together gives people the chance to get to know each other and to develop Christian friendships. It is important that the course is held in a welcoming environment.

Helping one another. The small groups encourage everyone to participate and help each other along the way, as they discuss the talks, study the Bible, and pray for each other. For the leaders and helpers, the course provides an opportunity to help bring others to faith. People often come back and help on the next course or bring their friends along to see what it is all about.

Ask anything. Alpha is a place where no question is regarded as too simple or too hostile. People are given a chance to raise their questions and discuss relevant topics in small groups after the talk.

There are many variables with Alpha courses including the size, location, and time of the course, as well as the number of people needed to run the course. Alpha courses vary in size. Some are very small and some are very large. Courses are held in homes, churches, prisons, and schools. The principles in this chapter apply to all courses regardless of size, location, or time. Since evening courses are most common, this model is explained in detail. If you are planning a daytime Alpha, read about evening Alpha and then go to page 41 where daytime Alpha is explained in depth. The expected attendance determines the number of people needed to run the course. Suggested organizational charts begin on page 32 and job descriptions begin on page 49.

EVENING ALPHA

Alpha is normally held at night when most people are available to attend. There are several important parts of evening Alpha—a simple dinner, a talk on some aspect of the Christian faith, informal interaction within preassigned small groups, a weekend away, and a celebration dinner which serves as the end of one course and the beginning of the next.

A typical evening

While the actual schedule may vary depending on location and day of the week, a typical evening will look something like this:

6:15 or 6:30 P.M.	Leaders and helpers meet to pray
7:00 P.M.	Dinner is served
7:40 P.M.	Welcome
7:50 P.M.	Songs of worship
8:00 P.M.	Talk
8:45 P.M.	Coffee
9:00 P.M.	Small groups
9:45 P.M.	End

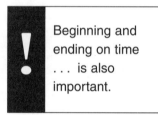

> ! Beginning and ending on time . . . is also important.

The meeting of the leaders and helpers at the beginning of the evening for prayer and organization is of great importance. Beginning and ending on time each week is also important.

Dinner.

Serve dinner at 7:00 P.M. Dinner is an important aspect of Alpha. People often feel more relaxed when visiting over a meal. Avoid "religious" conversation during dinner. The leaders and helpers should keep the conversation on personal, everyday things. This is a time to get to know the guests as individuals.

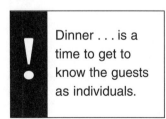

> ! Dinner . . . is a time to get to know the guests as individuals.

Often people have commented that the food kept them coming back to Alpha, so it is worth keeping the food at a high standard!

When Alpha is small (around twelve people), each person, starting with the leaders and helpers, can take turns cooking dinner. As it grows and there are up to about ten small groups, each small group can take a turn to cook. (Make sure you have enough paper plates and cups, coffee cups, knives, forks, spoons, tea, coffee, milk, and other beverages, etc.) If you don't have a Task Force (see page 57), the group who cooked should do the cleaning up and dishes.

Some suggestions for Alpha meals would include simple pasta dishes, sloppy joes, chili con carne, and pizza. Make sure you have a vegetarian alternative. Serve the main dish with a salad or gelatin, bread or rolls, and a simple dessert.

While there is no registration fee for the Alpha Course, it is reasonable to request a small contribution for the meal each evening. If a group is doing the cooking, the cost can usually be kept to approximately $3.00 to $5.00 per person. Place baskets for contributions at the serving points and reimburse whoever paid for the food. If you have a caterer, make the actual cost known and ask people to pay whatever they feel they can afford.

Eating together is an essential part of the course, as it gives people the chance to get to know others in a relaxed way. Friendships grow throughout the course, especially within the small groups, in an extraordinary way.

Welcome and worship.

At 7:40 P.M. welcome everyone and promote books and tapes related to that evening's talk. (Suggested titles are listed on pages 91-94 in this book and at the end of each session in *The Alpha Course Manual* and *Leader's Guide*). To help everyone relax, tell some kind of joke. Humor is an important part of the course and these jokes are usually appreciated out of all proportion to their merit! It is important for outsiders to see that Christians have a sense of humor and that laughter and faith in Jesus Christ are not incompatible. Beginning around Week 3 or 4 use this time to promote the weekend, and from Week 6 begin talking about the Celebration Dinner at the end of the course.

At 7:50 P.M. have a short period of singing. Make sure to explain carefully what you are going to do. I often quote what the apostle Paul says in his letter to the Ephesians, "Speak to one another with psalms, hymns and spiritual songs. Sing and make music in your heart to the Lord," (Eph. 5:19). I explain that we are going to sing a mixture of psalms (usually set to modern melodies), hymns, and spiritual songs. We have a mixture of old and new. We always start the first night with a well-known hymn for the benefit of those who might find that more familiar. As the course goes on we tend toward more modern songs, changing gradually from singing about God to singing directly to Him. We also increase the length of time we spend in worship from about five minutes on the first night to about fifteen to twenty minutes toward the end of the course. We try not to move too quickly at the beginning, and I explain that what matters is that we "sing and make music in our hearts". Some may not be ready to participate, so be sure to tell them that it is fine for them simply to listen until they are ready to join in.

The Worship Leader must sound confident, even if he or she is not. It is better that the Worship Leader give no introduction to the songs. This person is there to lead worship rather than to give what easily becomes another talk. Unless worship can be led and music played competently it is probably better not done at all. Some Alpha courses run without any singing. The very small courses who listen to the tapes or watch the video would not normally have any singing.

Although some guests find the singing the most difficult part of the course to begin with, and some are even hostile toward it, by the end they often find it is the part they value most. For many, such singing is their first experience of communicating with God. It also helps people to make the step from Alpha to the church where the worship of God is central.

The talk.

After the singing comes the talk. This may be given by the Alpha Leader or presented on videotape or DVD. (*The Alpha Course Videos* come in a set of five videotapes with three talks on each tape.) Because there are so many details to setting up an Alpha Course for the first time, many churches find it easiest to start with the talks on video and gradually shift to live speakers. In the long run this is probably best. On smaller courses it is probably better to have a variety of speakers. On larger ones it is necessary to have someone who is used to speaking to more sizable gatherings. This inevitably limits the number of speakers available. Chapter 6 of *Telling Others*[1] offers some insights on preparing and giving effective talks.

The talk for Week 1 is "Who Is Jesus?" (chapter 2 in *Questions of Life*[2] and *The Alpha Course Manual*; page 21 in *The Alpha Course Leader's Guide*). During Weeks 2–6 cover the material in chapters 3–7 of *Questions of Life*. The weekend away works best following Week 6; however, this may vary due to each individual situation. It is best to have the talk on God's guidance (#7) before the weekend away and before the talk titled "How Can I Resist Evil?" (#11). The talk about avoiding evil needs to always come after the weekend away. This is because the talk about spiritual warfare only becomes truly relevant after people have experienced the power of the Holy Spirit.

Following is a suggested sequence of fifteen Alpha talks. The number in parentheses after each title is the corresponding chapter in *Questions of Life* and *The Alpha Course Manual* and the corresponding talk on the *Alpha Course* videotapes.

WEEK	TITLE
1	Who Is Jesus? (#2)
2	Why Did Jesus Die? (#3)
3	How Can I Be Sure of My Faith? (#4)
4	Why and How Should I Read the Bible? (#5)
5	Why and How Do I Pray? (#6)
6	How Does God Guide Us? (#7)
WEEKEND AWAY	
	Who Is the Holy Spirit? (#8)
	What Does the Holy Spirit Do? (#9)
	How Can I Be Filled with the Spirit? (#10)
	How Can I Make the Most of the Rest of My Life? (#15)
7	How Can I Resist Evil? (#11)
8	Why and How Should We Tell Others? (#12)
9	Does God Heal Today? (#13)
10	What About the Church? (#14)
11	Celebration (or *Alpha*) Dinner; "Christianity: Boring, Untrue, and Irrelevant?" (#1)

The talk for Week 8 is "Why and How Should We Tell Others?" This is an excellent time to promote the Alpha dinner party or Celebration Dinner which is held at the end of the course (see page 31). Following the talk on healing (Week 9) there are no small groups due to a time of ministry (see chapter 7 in *Telling Others*).

For Week 10 the subject is the church. The main aim of this talk is to start integrating those who have been attending Alpha into the life of the church. If your church has ongoing small groups or home groups, encourage Alpha guests to join such a group. Often a whole small group from Alpha will join the same home group or small group.

Small groups.

At the end of the talk for Weeks 1–8 and 10, everyone meets in small groups (see chapter 5 in *Telling Others*). Each group should not exceed 12 people including two leaders and two helpers. It is important to end the groups promptly at 9:45 P.M. or the designated time. People need to know

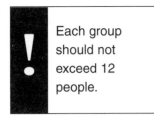

! Each group should not exceed 12 people.

when they can count on heading for home on time.

During the final small-group time, distribute a copy of the "Alpha Questionnaire" (see Section E, page 83) to each person and allow time to complete the questions before everyone leaves. Use the responses to these surveys to help you see how the course needs to be improved next time.

If you have people who are interested in Alpha but cannot attend during the evening, consider a daytime Alpha Course. Details are included beginning on page 41.

Resources and related reading.

The Church Leader needs to be very familiar with the content of *Telling Others,* especially chapters 4-6 which are used in training the Ministry Team. If the course leader is also giving the talks, he or she needs to master the content of *Questions of Life.*

The Director will use the information in this book to set up and run the course. Permission is granted to photocopy all of the sections in Part 3, but not the chapters in this book.

Each leader and helper (the Ministry Team) needs a copy of *Questions of Life, The Alpha Course Manual,* and *The Alpha Course Leader's Guide.* It is also helpful for each leader and even helpers to have access to a copy of this book and *Searching Issues* (contains answers to the seven most-asked questions during Alpha). Guests receive a copy of *Why Jesus?*[3] at the Alpha Dinner (or *Why Christmas?*[4] if it is Christmastime) and a copy of *The Alpha Course Manual* during Week 1. There is a list of related, recommended books at the end of each session in the manual and leader's guide (and on pages 91-94 in this book). These may be obtained from Christian bookstores or HTB. Ideally, a book table should be open for the whole evening (except during the talk) so that people may purchase any books they prefer. If the Alpha talk is given live by the Church Leader, ensure that the previous weeks' talks are available on audio tape so that anyone who misses a session can buy the tape. If you use *The Alpha Course DVDs* or *Videos,* have a set available for loan to those who may want to review or catch a missed talk.

The weekend

The weekend away is an essential part of the course. This time is devoted to teaching on the work of the Holy Spirit in the individual lives of those on the course. The material covered during the weekend is in chapters 8, 9, 10, and 15 of *Questions of Life* and Talks 8, 9, 10, and 15 on *The Alpha Course DVDs* or *Videos.* Also included on Video 3 is a short introduction to the weekend. If an entire weekend away is not feasible, it is possible to cover this material in a single day. Sometimes churches hold an all-day local weekend on a Saturday. However, there are tremendous advantages to the weekend away.

Friendships are formed over an entire weekend much more easily than on a single day. As people travel together, have meals together, go for walks, enjoy the Saturday night entertainment, and receive Communion together on Sunday morning, there is a cementing of friendships that have begun to form in the early weeks. It is in this relaxed environment that people unwind and some of the barriers begin to come down. Many make as much progress spiritually during the weekend away as in all the rest of the course put together.

Sometimes it is hard to find an affordable location, but it is usually possible if plans are made far enough ahead. If members of the congregation cannot afford the expense of an entire weekend at a retreat center or hotel, then the weekend could take place in a local setting. However, in most congregations those who can afford to pay are willing to help those who cannot by contributing all or a portion of the cost to a scholarship fund.

The following schedule is for a full weekend. For a Saturday-only schedule, combine talks 1 and 2 in the first session (see page 77).

FULL WEEKEND SCHEDULE

Friday

6:30 P.M. onward	Arrive
8:00 P.M.	Dinner or light supper
9:45 P.M.	Worship and a brief introduction to the weekend. This can include a short talk based on John 15 or perhaps a testimony.

Saturday

8:30 A.M.	Breakfast
9:00 A.M.	Leaders' meeting
9:30 A.M.	Worship Talk 1 - "Who Is the Holy Spirit?" *(on Video 3, #8)*
10:45 A.M.	Coffee
11:15 A.M.	Talk 2 - "What Does the Holy Spirit Do?" *(on Video 3, #9)*
12:00 P.M.	Small group discussion. Often we look at 1 Corinthians 12:1-11 and the subject of spiritual gifts. This gives people a chance to discuss and air their fears.
1:00 P.M.	Lunch
Free Afternoon	Activities can be organized, (for instance, sports, walks, etc.).
4:15 P.M.	Optional refreshments
5:00 P.M.	Worship Talk 3 - "How Can I Be Filled with the Spirit?" *(on Video 4, #10)*
7:00 P.M.	Dinner
8:30 P.M.	Optional - Talent Show *(A variety of skits and songs without anything distasteful, religious, or off- color. Participation is voluntary!)*

Sunday

9:00 A.M.	Breakfast
9:20 A.M.	Leaders' meeting
9:45 A.M.	Small group discussion. Often we talk about how each member of the group feels about the activities on Saturday.
10:30 A.M.	Worship Talk 4 - "How Can I Make the Most of the Rest of My Life?" *(on Video 5, #15)* Optional - Communion Service
1:00 P.M.	Lunch and Depart
Free Afternoon	Hopefully everybody meets again at the evening service at church!

More details about the weekend are included in the job descriptions for the Weekend Away Coordinator (*see page 63*) and the Weekend Entertainment Coordinator (*see page 65*).

The Celebration Dinner

The Alpha Celebration Dinner serves two purposes: it is the wrap-up for one course and the kickoff of the next course.

For your first Alpha Course, hold a dinner party before the course starts, then hold one at the end of every course so that guests on the course can invite their friends. You will begin to promote the dinner around Week 7 and at the same time start collecting money for the party. Everyone should pay for their guests as well as for themselves.

The Alpha Celebration Dinner wraps up one course and launches the next.

On Week 8 (when the talk is on "Why and How Should We Tell Others?"), advertise the dinner and give out the invitations. This will enable you to confirm the number of people coming by Week 10. When Alpha at Holy Trinity Brompton was small, each person would bring a certain amount of food. These days we use caterers, and those on the course contribute as they are able, bearing in mind the number of guests they intend to bring. If the number of people attending the Celebration Dinner exceeds a comfortable room capacity, consider holding two smaller dinners. We have been doing this at Holy Trinity Brompton for some time with great success. We have a dinner on each of the two Wednesdays following Week 10.

The Celebration Dinner begins at 7:00 P.M. when everyone gathers for beverages followed by a sit-down dinner together. To avoid embarrassing guests or making guests uncomfortable, we do not say grace.

All the details for the Celebration Dinner will be handled by a coordinator and team preferably made up of those who are not inviting friends. It is important to do everything possible to create a good atmosphere. Make a seating plan and set the tables with tablecloths, nice dinnerware, flowers, and candles. The talk should come after eating and during coffee. See the job description for the Alpha Dinner Coordinator on page 58 for more details about the Celebration Dinner.

At HTB, after a leisurely dinner, I welcome everyone. We usually thank those people who have organized the evening. I then invite one or two people who have attended the course to speak about what has happened in their lives, giving them a minimum of advance notice so that they do not have too long to worry about it. They are encouraged to speak from their hearts about their own experience, and the format is that of an interview.

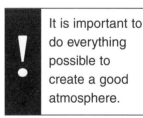

It is important to do everything possible to create a good atmosphere.

After the interview I give a talk along the lines of "Christianity: Boring, Untrue, and Irrelevant?" (chapter 1 in *Questions of Life;* Talk 1 in *The Alpha Course DVDs* or *Videos*). If the party is at Christmas, I give a similar talk but based around the theme "What Is the Point of Christmas?"

At the end of the talk I usually refer to Paul's experience in Athens where he found there was one of three reactions to what he had said about Jesus (see Acts 17: 32-34).

• "Some of them sneered." I point out that that was my own position for many years, so I am not judging them if they take the same position.

• Others said, "We want to hear you again on this subject" (vs. 32). I suggest that those who feel like that come to the next Alpha Course for which we have invitations and brochures are available.

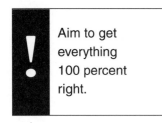

Aim to get everything 100 percent right.

• "A few . . . believed" (vs. 34). For the benefit of these, I ask everyone to bow their heads for a prayer and then I pray a prayer aloud along the lines of the one in the back of the booklet *Why Jesus?* There are usually some, I discover afterward, who pray the prayer that night.

I then encourage anyone interested to come to the first evening of the next Alpha Course at least. I offer every guest a copy of *Why Jesus?* or *Why Christmas?* as appropriate, and invite them to stay for coffee, dessert, and informal talking. Most of them stay and talk with the friends they came with and then the evening ends. Many of those who come to the supper wish to do an Alpha Course as soon as possible. Hence it is vital that there is one planned immediately thereafter.

The Alpha Dinner is one of the reasons why so many people come on each Alpha Course. We have found that each Alpha supper has been bigger than the one before and each Alpha Course likewise has been bigger than the one before. Therefore, it is good to make sure that people are organized to set tables, serve, and clean up, or chaos may ensue.

SETTING UP AND RUNNING THE ALPHA COURSE

There is a lot of hard work behind the scenes of an Alpha Course and every job is vitally important. Aim to get everything 100 percent right. Guests who come on the course will see that every effort has been made and that everything is run in an efficient way.

PREPARATION

It is essential to begin planning for your Alpha Course six to nine months in advance. This allows you to select and train an Alpha team and to promote the course effectively. A detailed timeline begins on page 69.

Some of the following information will apply only to larger courses, where the first thing the Church Leader should do is to appoint the Director *(or Administrator)*. The number of people needed to run an Alpha Course will vary depending on the number of expected guests.

Study the following sample organizational charts and adapt one to fit the number of guests or small groups you anticipate. Reproducible job descriptions for all positions begin on page 49.

SMALL ALPHA COURSES

For a course of fewer than twenty-five people *(or 1 or 2 small groups)*, the Church Leader and the Director usually run the entire program. The Church Leader either gives the talks or introduces the recorded talk each week and provides spiritual leadership, while the Director oversees the practical aspects such as the meal and weekend away. Both the Church Leader and the Director will lead or help lead a small group. Each person *(including the guests)* will take a turn preparing dinner. The organizational chart for this size ministry looks something like this:

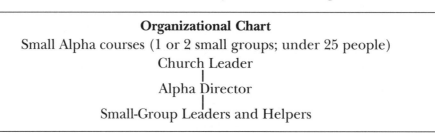

Organizational Chart
Small Alpha courses (1 or 2 small groups; under 25 people)
Church Leader
|
Alpha Director
|
Small-Group Leaders and Helpers

MEDIUM ALPHA COURSES

If you expect between 25 and 120 people *(or 3 to 9 groups),* adapt the following organizational chart to meet your needs. Director will serve as the Small Group Coordinator, while Task Force Members help greet, work at the book table *(we encourage you to have one),* serve and cleanup each week. The Ministry Team will be primarily the Small Group Leaders and Helpers along with the Church Leader and Director. The Alpha Director will coordinate the weekend away.

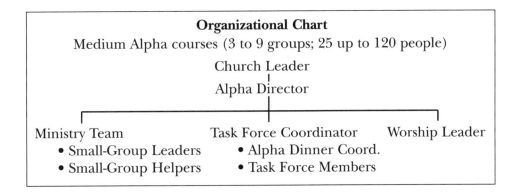

LARGE ALPHA COURSES

Once a course reaches 120 people (or ten small groups) or more, the work load increases significantly, so more workers are needed. Adapt the following chart to meet your needs. Because the weekend away involves a large number of people it is necessary to appoint a treasurer and weekend coordinator.

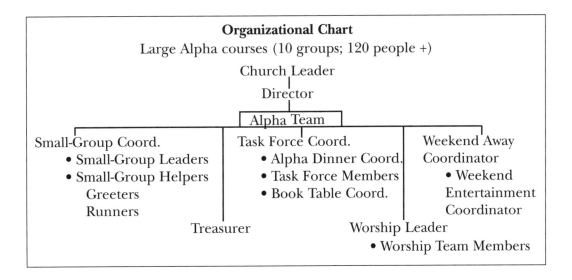

TEAM SELECTION

One of the most important aspects of an Alpha Course is the leadership team. It is vital to get the right people. Courses of all sizes need Small-Group Leaders and Helpers. You might first contact the small group or home group leaders of your church and ask them to suggest people who would

be good Alpha Small-Group Leaders and Helpers. It is important to emphasize commitment to the course, because if the leaders and helpers are not consistent in coming, then there is no reason why anybody else should come either.

SMALL-GROUP LEADERS

Approximately one-third of the course members should be leaders or helpers. Each small group is made up of around 12 people including three or four leaders and helpers who need to be selected very carefully. The leaders must be those who appear to have the beginnings of a gift of evangelism and are sensitive, encouraging, and easy to get along with. They do not necessarily need to be longtime Christians, but one indication of this gift of evangelism is that they are "good with people".

 Many helpers are those who have just finished the previous course.

Small-Group Helpers

Each small group also has one or two helpers, usually one man and one woman. They might be a couple or two single people. Try not to have a dating couple lead or help with the same group, as complications can arise if the relationship breaks up during the course. The ideal is to have one couple and two single people on the leadership team of each small group.

The helpers should pass the same test as the leaders but they may be relatively new Christians. Occasionally they may not even be Christians at all. Many helpers are those who have just finished the previous course. Some ask to come back and do the course again. In many cases I would ask them to come back as helpers. People who have recently done the course are often especially sensitive to the fears and doubts of members of their group. They can empathize with them, saying, "I felt that way too," or "I found that difficult." This removes the "we" and "they" barrier.

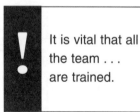 It is vital that all the team . . . are trained.

Ask the leaders of the previous course to recommend small-group members who would be good at helping. Watch for those who would make good helpers and ask them to come back and help. Many of them are new Christians and many have lots of friends who are not Christians. Quite a high percentage of the next course will be friends of those who are helping. This is one of the ways in which the course grows.

TASK FORCE

It is helpful to have a Task Force to perform practical tasks such as greeting, setting up, serving, and cleaning up. This group is vital to the smooth running of the course. In this way very few people from the course will be asked to help with the more mundane tasks and will therefore not be distracted from their enjoyment of Alpha. The Task Force should be welcome to listen to the talks and should be given as much encouragement as possible. Always cherish your Task Force!

At Holy Trinity Brompton we have a remarkable group on the Task Force. They are people who either do not want to be in a small group or would not be suitable as Small-Group Leaders or Helpers but have "the gift of helps" (from 1 Cor. 12:28). They are like the group chosen in the Book of Acts to "wait on tables" (Acts 6: 2). They are men and women who are full of the Spirit and willing to serve in any capacity. Their love and service alone are a powerful witness of the love of Christ to those who are on the course. A key appointment is the Task Force Coordinator who assigns tasks and offers pastoral care. A full job description for this person is on page 55 in Section A.

TEAM TRAINING

It is vital that all the team (including those who have been Christians for many years) are trained. Insist that all leaders and helpers come to the training sessions. If they are unable to come, ask them to listen to the tape or view the video. Even if some of your team have helped on several Alpha courses, they should come to every training session of every course. Even if one of your leaders has been leading small groups for twenty years or so, stress that Alpha small groups are very different.

Small-Group Leaders and Helpers and Task Force Members attend three training sessions as follows:

Two weeks prior to course	Session 1	Leading Small Groups
One week prior to course	Session 2	Pastoral Care
Week prior to weekend away	Session 3	Ministry during Alpha

The content of these three training sessions is contained in chapters 4, 5, and 7 of *Telling Others,* Part I of *The Alpha Course Leader's Guide,* and the entirety of *The Alpha Leader's Training DVD* or *Video.* Training sessions run similarly to evening Alpha:

7:00 P.M.	Dinner
7:45 P.M.	Worship and prayer
8:00 P.M.	Training talk
9:00 P.M.	Discussion of talk
10:00 P.M.	End of training

It is recommended that all leaders and helpers read three books before the course begins: *Questions of Life, Searching Issues,* and *Telling Others.* It is important that the team members spend time together and get to know each other before the course begins. Do not assume that they already know each other very well. After the training talk give an opportunity to ask questions either relating to the talk or about any other aspect of the Alpha Course. At this point cover some of the administrative details and prepare people for the jobs they will be asked to do on the first evening and thereafter. Job descriptions for all positions are included in Section A beginning on page 49.

! It is best to put together a team who will work well with one another.

Throughout the training and the course, stress the importance of praying for every aspect of Alpha. Ask the leaders and helpers to commit themselves to pray for every member of their group regularly.

Emphasize to all leaders, helpers, and Task Force Members that their commitment is not just for eleven weeks (including the

Celebration Dinner) but also for three training nights. Leaders and helpers will also need to commit to social evenings with their group, follow-up after the course has finished, getting group members into an ongoing small group or home group, and integrating them into the church.

SMALL-GROUP ASSIGNMENTS

This can be a very challenging task, so allow plenty of time. Be firm with your team, emphasizing that everyone should be willing to do anything from leading to cleanup.

Arrange groups primarily by age and think carefully about the dynamics of the group: the balance of personalities, social backgrounds, professions, etc. If your church has home groups or other small groups, it is also good to select a team from the same group so that there can be continuity for the guests after the Alpha Course. Regardless, it is best to put together a team who will work well with one another. Allocate a specific person in each group to look after the administration for their group, preferably someone who is gifted in that area and who can definitely come to the administration/prayer meetings prior to Alpha every week.

Often you will have very little information about your guests. From the registration form you may only have their name, address, telephone number, an idea of their age, and their handwriting!

Remember that these are individuals. At Holy Trinity we pray over almost every single registration and ask for guidance. If people are not happy in their groups, they might not come back, so it is very important to get it right. If there is a genuine reason why someone should move to a different group (such as a large age gap with the rest of the group), do it in the first week. Otherwise it is disruptive for those in the original group as well as the new one.

If a guest is a friend of someone on the team, try to find out as much as possible about the guest which will help you to put them in the right group. Quite often it is better not to put the guest in the same group as a friend who is helping as he or she often feels inhibited and unable to ask questions. Always put married couples in the same group unless specifically asked to do otherwise.

Aim to finalize this task on the last day before the course starts. In this way last-minute applications will be on your list, assigned a group, and have a preprinted name tag.

SET UP ACCOUNTING SYSTEM

The financing of the Alpha Course, and particularly of the Alpha Weekend/Day should be a matter of prayer. Begin developing a budget for the:
- Introductory Alpha supper (before your first Alpha Course)
- Weekly Alpha sessions
- Alpha Celebration Supper party (following each Alpha Course)
- Alpha Weekend/Day away

For example, you will need to think about the cost of: invitations and Alpha brochures, postage, food, Alpha manuals, other course resources, training resouces, and more.

Meet with the church treasurer to learn about church policies concerning handling money. Check on insurance coverage and make arrangements for coverage for all aspects of the course as needed. For larger courses you may wish to appoint a treasurer.

WIN THE SUPPORT OF YOUR CONGREGATION

You will find most people attend the Alpha Course because they have been invited by a friend. Therefore, your congregation is the best advertisement for the Alpha Course. It is important that they be informed and challenged about the course in order for it to become an effective evangelistic tool in your church.

The following are suggestions as to how you might achieve this:

- You could run the first Alpha Course for the congregation, so they will feel comfortable inviting their unchurched friends to the next course.
- Invite your Alpha Regional Advisor to give a presentation to your congregation about the Alpha Course, or show *The Alpha Introductory Video.*
- Circulate copies of *Alpha News.*
- Include Alpha testimonies in your church newsletter.
- Encourage your congregation to invite friends and family to the Introductory Alpha Supper before your first course.
- Encourage your congregation to invite friends an family to an Alpha Guest Service before the course starts.

TAP INTO ADDITIONAL RESOURCES

The Alpha Conference

Many churches have found it helpful to attend an Alpha conference before running their own Alpha Course. Alpha conferences are held throughout North America and in many other countries around the world. The purpose of an Alpha conference is to expose interested church staff and laypersons to the ministry of Alpha and to help them understand the principles and practicalities of setting up and running an Alpha Course. For information about upcoming conferences, in the United States call toll free: 1-866-US-ALPHA (1-866-872-5742), or visit the Alpha North American website: www.alphana.org.

The first two sessions of an Alpha conference are available on videotape (*How to Run the Alpha Course Video*).

Contact Your Alpha Advisor

We have established a support network of Alpha Advisors to help you to both set up and sustain your Alpha Course. Each advisor has experience in running Alpha Courses in his or her area. You will find contact details for your Alpha Advisor in *Alpha News*. (See the following for how to register and receive your copy of *Alpha News.*)

Your Alpha Advisor will not only provide you with answers to your general questions about the Alpha Course, but may also be able to:

- Suggest speakers to give a presentation about Alpha to your church governing body.
- Suggest locations in your area for an Alpha Weekend or Day Away.
- Suggest speakers for your Introductory Supper at the beginning of your first Alpha Course or Alpha Celebration Supper.
- Suggest speakers and a ministry team to support you on your Alpha Weekend/Day Away.
- Run training days for your Alpha team.

Please do not hesitate to contact your Advisor. He or she will be delighted to help you.

Register Your Alpha Course

There are a number of benefits to registering your Alpha Course. Your listing will appear in the Alpha Register, a list of all the Alpha courses running world-wide which have been registered with an Alpha office. This listing is updated regularly and published in *Alpha News* and on the Internet. We receive a number of calls each week from people wanting to be directed to a course in their area. Using the Register, people can find courses not only for themselves, but also for their friends and family.

By registering your course, you will regularly receive a copy of *Alpha News,* and you will also be informed about special events that may be taking place.

To register, simply contact your national Alpha office for a registration form (see information below), complete the form available in *Alpha News,* or register online.

YOUR ALPHA OFFICE

For more information about anything to do with the Alpha Course, just contact:

Alpha U.S.A.
74 Trinity Place
New York, NY 10006
Tel: 888.949.2574
Fax: 212.406.7521
e-mail: info@alphausa.org
www.alphausa.org

Alpha Canada
1620 W. 8th Ave, Suite 300
Vancouver, BC V6J 1V4
Tel: 800.743.0899
Fax: 604.224.6124
e-mail: office@alphacanada.org
www.alphacanada.org

To purchase resources in Canada:

Cook Communications Ministries
P.O. Box 98, 55 Woodslee Avenue
Paris, ONT N3L 3E5
Tel: 800.263.2664
Fax: 800.461.8575
e-mail: custserv@cook.ca
www.cook.ca

THE FIRST COURSE

It is vitally important to decide who will be invited to attend the first course. Is your purpose to reach those on the fringe of the church from the first course on? Or is it initially to expose the church members to the Alpha ministry and then reach out beyond your active membership?

If you answer yes to the first question, the way to start is simply to begin with a small group of anyone interested and allow it to grow from there. If you want everyone in the church to experience Alpha, you will start with a large course introducing Alpha to the whole church.

Either option is valid as long as your expectations meet the likely results. Experience has shown that with option one, the numbers start small and gradually build. With the second option, the numbers begin large, drop off for a time, and then rebuild gradually.

It is important to remember that ideally Alpha is an ongoing ministry of evangelism. It may take a few courses to work out the details of getting started and for church members to gain the confidence to invite their friends or associates. At the beginning stages it is important to persevere and not be discouraged if the numbers drop. In time, the effect of new Christians reaching their friends has a ripple effect and the numbers begin to grow.

 Remember that ideally Alpha is an ongoing ministry of evangelism.

Dates

The next step to an effective Alpha Course is to set the dates. Make sure that your Alpha Course does not conflict with anything that will keep people from coming, such as Thanksgiving, the Christmas holidays, Easter, or summer vacations. Remember to allow enough time for the two training sessions before the course begins and the Celebration Dinner at the end of the course. The best times are:

- Fall session (late September or early October through early December),
- Winter session (January through March or between Christmas and Easter), and
- Spring session (April through early June or after Easter).

It is best for the fall session to finish a week or two before Christmas, the winter session to begin a week or two after Christmas and finish before Easter, and the spring session to end before schools are out for the summer.

The course takes eleven weeks (including the Alpha Dinner at the beginning of your first Alpha Course or the Celebration Dinner party at the end of each subsequent course). Alpha at Holy Trinity Brompton takes place on Wednesday evenings. Another option is a daytime Alpha as described on pages 41-43 in this book. If you are doing daytime Alpha, tie in the course with the school calendar. It is of utmost importance, in order to maintain the momentum, to run at least three courses a year. When people complete Alpha they very often want to invite their families and friends to the next course, and it is important that one is available.

Location

To start, the ideal meeting place is a home because such an environment is unthreatening for those who do not go to church. For many years the Alpha Course at Holy Trinity Brompton was run in a home, and we had considerable hesitations about moving to a different setting. We only did so eventually because of the increasing size of the course. When the course outgrows the home, a new location with a welcoming atmosphere needs to be found. If the course is held in a church, it is best to meet in a room other than the sanctuary or worship center. Those who are unchurched are most comfortable in a neutral setting, such as an auditorium.

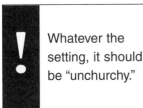 Whatever the setting, it should be "unchurchy."

Whatever the setting, it should be "unchurchy." It can often be difficult to make a church hall look welcoming. If you must use the church remember these tips:

- Use standard lamps instead of overhead fluorescent lighting.
- Provide flowers.
- Cover unattractive tables.

- Adjust temperature.
- Arrange the chairs so that guests can eat together in their groups.
- Make sure that there is good lighting on the speaker and that everyone is able to hear. This may involve arranging a PA system.
- Provide space to hang coats and a secure place for briefcases, purses, and other bags.
- Display signs for directions to rest rooms, book sales, and small-group locations.

Promotion

Promotion of the Alpha Course is important so that those outside the church and those on its fringes can be attracted. This can be done through brochures, during worship services on special "Alpha Sundays," and at the Celebration Dinner at the end of the course. Once the congregation has confidence in the course they will invite their friends.

Brochure. A quality registration brochure accompanied by a letter is an effective method of promotion. Either prepare an attractive brochure with all the relevant details or purchase packets of fifty full-color brochures with instructions for customizing them for your Alpha Course from the publisher (see page 94 for ordering information). If you create your own brochure, permission is granted to reproduce the Alpha logo. Alternatively, produce a simple letter which sets out all the dates with a tear-off slip at the bottom.

Fringe. Many people within a church have friends who attend only occasionally, perhaps only on holidays. These people on the fringe are prime candidates to attend Alpha. At our church, we also encourage adults who are preparing for baptism, parents wanting to have their children baptized,

! The best people to interview are those who do not volunteer.

and confirmation candidates to do the course. I even encourage couples who are intending to get married in the church to attend Alpha as part of their marriage preparation. Some have said to me that it was the best possible marriage preparation as it transformed not only their relationship with God but also their relationship with each other. We would also advertise the course at services which attract those on the fringe, such as the services at Christmas and Easter.

Guest Services/Alpha Sundays. Designate the two Sundays prior to the beginning of the Alpha Course as "Alpha Sundays." At Holy Trinity Brompton the first Sunday is a regular service with a testimony advertising Alpha. I explain what Alpha is (using the mnemonic at the start of this chapter). Then I interview someone who has just done the course. I choose someone with whom people will find it easy to identify and about whom they cannot say, "I can see why he or she needs Christianity, but it's not for me." In an interview I normally ask them to say something about what they felt about Christianity before the course, what happened to them, and the changes it has made in their lives. I ask them to avoid glittering generalizations. Rather they should be specific and give concrete examples of the changes that have occurred.

The best people to interview are those who do not volunteer. This is because if they agree, then they are only speaking for the benefit of others and not for themselves. Ask people about ten minutes beforehand. If they are asked any further in advance they begin to write things down and the interview loses its freshness and power. In those ten minutes ask them the same questions you will really ask them later. This gives you a chance to pick up on anything interesting and it allows them a chance to practice. I also give them lots of reassurance that all will be well!

The second Sunday is a guest service which is designed especially for church members to invite their friends and family. This service is low-key and the sermon is evangelistic and challenging. Again Alpha would be advertised and a testimony heard. Alpha brochures and complimentary copies of *Why Jesus?* are given to everyone at the end.

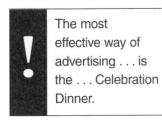

The most effective way of advertising . . . is the . . . Celebration Dinner.

These services are designed to make it easy for people to bring their friends who would not normally go to church. Keep the service short and specifically aim the talk at the questions often raised by non-Christians such as "What is the meaning of life?" or "Isn't Christianity a crutch?" At the end of the talk suggest that those who would like to investigate Christianity further come along to Alpha. Be careful not to ask them to identify themselves as most of those who are not used to going to church wish to remain anonymous.

I suggest they come along to the first night of Alpha. I tell them that if they don't want to come back after that first night, no one is going to call them or send them junk mail. This takes the pressure off them. Most who come to the first night continue to come of their own accord.

Celebration Dinner. The most effective way of advertising an Alpha Course is through the Celebration Dinner at the end of the course. This provides an opportunity for guests to invite their friends and families to see what they have been doing for the last ten weeks. It is helpful to encourage people to think about who they will invite to the closing dinner as early as Week 6 or 7. See page 31 for more details about the Celebration Dinner.

DAYTIME ALPHA[5]

Daytime Alpha is held on a weekday morning and was originally designed for those who found it easier to attend a course during the day. There are several groups of people who attend including mothers of young children, those who are self-employed or unemployed, and those who prefer not to venture out alone at night. At Holy Trinity Brompton this has generally been a group for women, but recently each group included more men.

The daytime Alpha Course has proved as successful as the evening course as a means of evangelism. This course, with its appeal to both the head and the heart, has seen many people come into relationship with Christ—from those very far away from Christianity to those who have sat in pews in churches for much of their lives but have not understood that the heart of the Christian faith is a relationship with Jesus. One team member, who had brought about twelve people from her own church to do the morning course at Holy Trinity Brompton, said at the end of the ten weeks that she had sat for years in the church with these people and none of them had moved in any real way toward conversion. Now, many had been converted during the course and they all wanted to attend another Alpha Course.

As with evening Alpha, we use an simple acronym to help people understand Alpha. This one is just slightly different.

Anyone can come.
Laughing, learning, and lunch.
Prayer.
Helping one another.
Ask anything.

A typical morning

Specific times will vary from one daytime Alpha Course to another. It is important to allow enough time for small-group discussion after the talk and to make sure the schedule coordinates with local school times.

A schedule for daytime Alpha will look something like this:

10:00 A.M.	Child care opens
10:20 A.M.	Welcome & coffee
	Worship
10:30 A.M.	Talk
11:15	Additional short coffee break
11:30 A.M.	Small Groups
12:00	Finish

Values. The daytime Alpha Course promotes the same values as the evening Alpha with some small differences of emphasis, resulting from the time of the meeting and particularly from the ministry of "women to women." The main two values are:
- Lead the guests to a personal relationship with God through Jesus Christ.
- Love the lost, lonely, and unhappy.

Anyone may come, at any stage of their life and from any background. As with evening Alpha it is very important to make people feel welcome. Try to foster relationships in a relaxed atmosphere. Once during the ten weeks, plan lunch together as part of the course. It is very often a sign of the groups jelling together and friendships being formed when groups begin to arrange to have lunch together after the course is over.

Today many women take some kind of course in the morning—art, history, languages, etc.— so they can be encouraged to come and learn about the Christian faith. We also find that many, even those who are not Christians, have been crying out to God for their needs and those of their family (without knowing Him or His power to change things). As a consequence, they readily understand about prayer and begin to pray together early in the course.

The main difference in the organization and timing of daytime Alpha is the absence of the weekend away. It is often not practical for women to be separated from their families over an entire weekend. A good alternative is a day beginning with coffee at 9 A.M., followed by worship and a talk on "How Can I Be Filled with the Spirit?" which will combine three talks in one (chapters 8, 9, and 10 in *Questions of Life*). Include a time of ministry after the talk and then have lunch. Allow time for small groups where the guests can raise questions or the group can have time for more prayer. Make sure everything is over in time for moms to get their children after school.

Small groups. Most guests tend to enjoy the small groups more than anything else. They often come needing love, acceptance, and forgiveness and they find it in their groups. Some come with damaged lives from abuse of all kinds. Many need a place of peace where they can learn to accept God's forgiveness for those things they have done of which they feel ashamed, and where they can learn to trust God and to forgive those who have hurt them. We try to group people of similar age and location together. Mothers enjoy being with others who have children of a similar age, as it means they all have similar joys and problems.

> Guests tend to enjoy the small groups more than anything else.

Daytime Alpha dinner. As with evening Alpha, hold a special Celebration Dinner. This dinner party at the end of the course is an excellent setting for married women to bring their husbands who oftentimes have been very pleasantly surprised at some of the changes in the lives of their spouses. The dinner gives husbands or other guests a wonderful opportunity to hear the Gospel in a relaxed environment. It has been one of the striking features of daytime Alpha that many of the husbands have gone on to do an evening Alpha and have come to know Christ. Women who are not married are encouraged to bring their friends to the dinner party.

Location. As with evening Alpha, daytime Alpha probably works best meeting in a home until the group gets too large. It can work very well in a church hall or similar building, providing there is room for child care.

MORNING ALPHA

September 27th – December 6th

We invite you to join the new Morning Alpha Course

beginning on September 27th

The course runs for ten weeks on Wednesday morning

from 10:00 a.m. to 12 noon at (location).

The mornings provide time for a talk on Christian basics, followed by

a break for coffee, discussion groups, and an opportunity to ask questions. There will be a

special half-day with lunch on November 8th

when the talk will be "How Can I Be Filled with the Spirit?"

– further details later.

The course is ideal for anyone who wants to learn more about

the Christian faith and/or anyone who would like to inquire into what

Christianity really means.

It is a wonderful opportunity to meet new people and make new friends.

Child care is available.

Numbers. The course seems to work equally well whatever the numbers. We have done courses from twenty people to two hundred with the Lord working in equal power in people's lives.

Invitations and schedule. We suggest a letter or invitation card inviting people to join the morning Alpha Course, telling them how long the course is to run and the schedule of the morning. For example:

Team selection

Small-Group Leaders and Helpers. The priorities are the same as for an evening Alpha: choosing people who have vision for what the course can do, choosing new Christians who have many friends who do not know Christ, and training them to be helpers for the next course. It is possible to have smaller groups with the daytime Alpha (maybe eight or even six people per group). There should be two team members or leaders and one helper to each group.

Task Force. It is important to be well organized and to have someone from among the helpers who will organize the coffee for each morning, set out chairs, organize child care, and be responsible for arranging the lunch. There should also be a prayer task force who meet together for prayer half an hour before the morning begins. All the team will be committed to praying, but with the various school starting times and other morning commitments it is not always possible for all the team to meet beforehand.

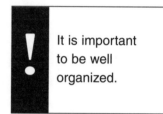

It is important to be well organized.

Ask the leaders and helpers to make the following commitments:
- Attend the entire course and all training sessions.
- Be on time.
- Pray for all aspects of Alpha (the speaker, the small groups, the guests, etc.)
- Prepare thoroughly for each session.

All leaders and helpers need to attend two training sessions: one before the course begins and one before the one-day weekend away. The first session will cover Leading Small Groups and Pastoral Care (Sessions 1 & 2 in *The Alpha Leader's Training DVD* or *Video*). The second training session will cover Ministry during Alpha (Session 3 of *The Alpha Leader's Training DVD* or *Video*).

Results

During the years that we have had a daytime Alpha, we have had many wonderful conversions and healings. We have often found that after only a few weeks of the course whole families are coming to church.

AFTER ALPHA

In practice, the strong friendships often formed on Alpha mean that the small groups want to stay together afterward. However, new Christians need to be integrated into the life of the Christian community, and the appropriate ways of doing this will vary.

Before you start your course, you may want to think about how you will encourage those who have completed the course to develop their faith. This can be done in a number of ways. You may like to integrate those completing the course into existing home groups or choose to establish new ones. Alternatively, you might run a follow-up course based on the Alpha model.

All of these courses are available as books with study guides, videos, and manuals.

- *A Life Worth Living* (Nine studies in the Book of Philippians)
- *Searching Issues* (Seven studies on the most asked questions during Alpha)
- *Challenging Lifestyle* (A two-term course based on the teachings of Jesus in the Sermon on the Mount.)
- *The Heart of Revival* (Ten Bible studies based on Isaiah 40-66, drawing out important truths for today.)

These can be obtained from your Alpha supplier. See Section G, pages 91-92.

SECRETS OF SUCCESS

PRAYER

For the leader or helper on Alpha it is impossible to exaggerate the importance of prayer. At the prayer meeting before every weekly session of the course we pray about the worship, the talk, the small groups, the general atmosphere, the administration, the weekend, and the dinner party(ies) at the end. In addition I ask them to pray for those in their small groups as often as they can. There seems to be a direct correlation between the amount of prayer and the fruitfulness of the small groups. Groups which have borne lasting fruit have always had at least one helper who was strongly committed to praying for each member of the group.

> ! New Christians need to be integrated into the Christian community.

PERSONAL CARING

The leaders and helpers need to get to know each person in the group. It is important to learn their names on the first night. Sometimes we play a name game to make this easier. Each evening of the course the group sits together for supper and the leaders and helpers act as hosts and facilitate the conversations. Sometimes the group will go out together at the end of the evening. Sometimes they will meet up during the week, either on a one-to-one basis or as a group with everyone together.

ENCOURAGEMENT

People need to feel it is safe to raise their honest questions. A good leader will always be an encourager. At the most basic level this means smiling at people, being interested in what each person has to say, and showing an interest in each person. It is important to give everyone an opportunity to ask questions about the talk.

COMMITMENT

On the evenings themselves it is important for the helpers and leaders of each group to get together to talk and pray for their group and also to discuss the ways of overcoming any problems within it. It is essential that the Alpha Team consistently attend all sessions and the weekend away. In this way, the team subtly emphasizes the importance of the course.

NOTES

1. Nicky Gumbel, *Telling Others* (New York, NY: Alpha North America, 2002).

2. Nicky Gumbel, *Questions of Life* (Colorado Springs, CO: Cook Communications Ministries, 1996).

3. Nicky Gumbel, *Why Jesus?* (Alpha North America).

4. Nicky Gumbel, *Why Christmas?* (Alpha North America).

5. The information about daytime Alpha was originally developed by Deidre Hurst. She has run daytime Alpha at Holy Trinity Brompton Church in London for many years as well as leading Alpha Courses in other parts of England.

Part III
Resources

Alpha

Alpha Course Job Descriptions

This Section includes job descriptions for the positions listed below. Note that positions vary by size of the Alpha Course as suggested on pages 32-33. Small courses are defined as 1 or 2 small groups (or up to 25 people); medium courses as 3 to 9 small groups (or 25 to 120 people); and large courses as 10 or more small groups (or more than 120 people).

These job descriptions are included to help you organize your Alpha Course. Do not feel that you need to structure exactly as suggested. Adapt the job descriptions as needed to fit the size of your course and the talents of your team.

Church Leader (all courses regardless of size)

Director (all courses regardless of size)

Alpha Team

   Small-Group Coordinator (larger medium and large courses)

   Small-Group Leaders

   Small-Group Helpers

   Task Force Coordinator (larger medium and large courses)

   Alpha Dinner Coordinator (larger medium and large courses)

   Task Force Members (medium and large courses)

   Book Table Coordinator (larger medium and large courses)

   Treasurer

   Worship Leader (all but the smallest courses)

   Weekend Away Coordinator

   Alpha Weekend Entertainment Coordinator

Church Leader

The Church Leader is responsible for the spiritual leadership for the entire Alpha ministry. Spiritual leadership is provided for the Director, all members of the Alpha Team (all course coordinators, Small-Group Leaders and Helpers, and Worship and Task Force Members), and the guests.

Qualifications

A spiritually mature Christian who has a heart for the lost; understands and agrees with the philosophy and theology of the Alpha ministry; understands the work of the Holy Spirit; is "full of the Spirit and wisdom" (Acts 6:3); is good with people; and is gifted in the areas of leadership, teaching, discernment, healing, or faith.

Specific Responsibilities

1. Provide spiritual leadership for all aspects of the Alpha ministry including team training, weekly sessions, ministry times, and the weekend away.

2. Provide guidance for all practical aspects of the Alpha ministry as needed.

3. Determine with the church staff and Alpha Team whether the talks will be presented live or via videotape. If live, determine who will give each talk. (The Alpha Leader will usually present the majority of the talks.)

4. In conjunction with the Small-Group Coordinator, select all Small-Group Leaders and Small-Group Helpers.

5. Be sensitive to the spiritual and emotional needs of the Alpha Team and Alpha guests. Offer pastoral care as needed.

6. Prepare for each worship time by praying for the speaker (if someone other than yourself), the Alpha Worship Leader, the Alpha Team Members, the guests, and yourself. Ask the Holy Spirit to reveal any area of your life where you need forgiveness and to fill you.

7. Be familiar with the philosophy of pastoral care and ministry during Alpha. Principles and methods of pastoral care are included in chapter 5 of *Telling Others,* and Session 2 of *The Alpha Leader's Training Video* or *DVD.* Ministry during Alpha is covered in chapter 7 of *Telling Others,* and Session 3 of *The Alpha Leader's Training Video* or *DVD.*

8. Impart these principles and vision of the Alpha Ministry to the Alpha Team through three training sessions. The first two sessions (Leading Small Groups and Pastoral Care) will be held during the two weeks immediately preceding the course. The third session (Ministry during Alpha) will be held one week prior to the weekend away.

9. During the ministry times, pray for those who respond and indicate they would like prayer. Ministry times are included during the weekend away and following the talk "Does God Heal Today?" Remember the guidelines to pray in teams with a designated leader and to pray for members of your same sex.

10. Model spiritual leadership by being available to all team members, praying for them regularly, and consistently affirming them.

11. Represent the Alpha ministry in all church committee and board meetings.

Director (or Administrator)

The Director is responsible—with the help of the Alpha Team and Alpha Task Force—for all the practical aspects of setting up and running an Alpha Course including all phases of Alpha (the Alpha Dinner, the 10 weekly sessions, the Alpha Weekend, and the Celebration Dinner). The Director's amount of involvement with the specific details of Alpha will vary by the size of the course. In smaller courses the Director will have more hands-on involvement, and as a course grows, this person will delegate more to an Alpha leadership team as detailed in the suggested following job descriptions.

Qualifications

A spiritually mature Christian who has a heart for the lost; understands and agrees with the philosophy and theology of the Alpha ministry; sees Alpha as an ongoing ministry, not a onetime event; and possesses gifts in the area of leadership, administration, and helps.

Specific Responsibilities

1. Oversee the planning and running of the Alpha Course.

2. Assist the Church Leader in selecting an Alpha Team as needed depending on course size.

3. Schedule monthly planning and prayer meetings with all coordinators and team leaders. Report progress to the Church Leader.

4. Work with the Church Leader to provide team members with training, clear instructions, and deadlines for their areas of responsibility.

5. Encourage team members to prepare for the ministry times and each session with prayer.

6. During the course conduct weekly administration and prayer meeting. For larger courses, this responsibility can be delegated to the Small-Group Coordinator.

7. Model spiritual leadership by being available to all team members, praying for them regularly, and consistently affirming them.

8. With the Book Table Coordinator, determine quantity of all course materials (*The Alpha Course Manual* and *Leader's Guide, Why Jesus?* or *Why Christmas? Questions of Life,* and *How to Run the Alpha Course*) and related reading (see complete listing on pages 91-94).

9. Order and maintain an adequate quantity of Alpha resources and related reading. (See page 94 for ordering information.) In larger courses, oversee the Book Table Coordinator who will order and maintain resources for the book table.

10. If using *The Alpha Course Videos,* make sure videos 3, 4, and 5 are available at the Weekend Away.

11. Conduct an evaluation of the ministry with the help of the Alpha Team and the "Alpha Questionnaire" (see page 83).

12. Schedule a post Alpha evaluation meeting. Based on the completed questionnaires, determine necessary changes and adjustments to increase the effectiveness of the Alpha ministry.

The Small-Group Coordinator

Serves as a member of the Alpha Team and reports to the Director.

The key responsibility of this person is to recruit, oversee, and encourage Small-Group Leaders and Helpers.

Qualifications

Experienced in facilitating small-group interaction; organized; able to encourage others; understands that the purpose of the small groups during Alpha is to provide a safe place for non-Christians to interact and respond to the talks; has good interpersonal skills; sensitive; gifted in areas of hospitality and evangelism; and has a servant's heart.

Specific Responsibilities

1. With the Church Leader and Director, select Small-Group Leaders and Helpers. When recruiting leaders, ask, "If I had a non-churchgoing friend for whom I had been praying for years, would I be totally confident about putting him or her in _____'s group?"

2. Attend all training sessions, the opening Alpha Dinner, all weekly administrative/ prayer meetings, each of 10 weekly Alpha sessions, the weekend away, any follow-up meetings, and the Celebration Dinner.

3. Model spiritual leadership by being available to all Small-Group Leaders and Helpers, praying for them regularly, and affirming them consistently.

4. Remind leaders and helpers that they do not have to "teach"; rather, they are to create a welcoming atmosphere where guests feel free to ask honest questions about the Christian faith.

5. With the Alpha Director, assign all leaders, helpers, and guests to small groups.

6. Make sure each group has enough copies of *The Alpha Course Manual.*

7. Encourage leaders and helpers to begin praying for their group members as soon as assignments are made and daily thereafter.

8. Emphasize to all leaders and helpers the importance of commitment to the course.

The Small-Group Leaders

Serve as part of the Ministry Team and report to the Small-Group Coordinator.

The key responsibility of the Small-Group Leader is to facilitate discussion in the small groups and to create a welcoming atmosphere where guests feel free to ask honest questions about the Christian faith.

Qualifications

A growing Christian; has at least the beginnings of the gift of evangelism; is good with people; sensitive; understands the work of the Holy Spirit; is "full of the Spirit and wisdom" (Acts 6:3); understands from where nonchurchgoers or non-Christians are coming; nonjudgmental; and has a servant's heart.

Specific Responsibilities

1. Attend all training sessions, the opening Alpha Dinner, all weekly administrative/prayer meetings, each of 10 weekly Alpha sessions, the weekend away, any follow-up meetings, and the Celebration Dinner.

2. Read *Questions of Life* and *Searching Issues* (both by Nicky Gumbel) prior to Alpha to become familiar with the course content and objections to the Christian faith which may arise during the course.

3. Prepare for each small-group time by reviewing the material and praying for the speaker, the other leaders and helpers, and each group member. Be prepared to lead a Bible study when your group is ready and as outlined in *The Alpha Course Leader's Guide.*

4. Be familiar with the material in chapter 5 of *Telling Others* and pages 18–44 of *The Alpha Course Leader's Guide.* If at all possible do not have the Leader's Guide in plain view during group time, especially during the early sessions. You want group members to discuss freely and not to feel you are following a script.

5. Be sensitive to the spiritual and emotional needs of all Alpha participants. Offer pastoral care as needed.

6. Prepare for each worship time by praying for the speaker, the Worship Leader, other Worship and Ministry Team Members, the guests, and yourself. Ask the Holy Spirit to reveal any area of your life where you need forgiveness and to fill you.

7. During the ministry times, pray for those who respond and indicate they would like prayer. Ministry times follow Talks 9 and 12. Remember the guidelines to pray in teams with a designated leader and to pray for members of your same sex.

Reminders for leading effective small groups

1. Become a facilitator (simply another member of the group who is helping to make the discussion happen). Seek to guide and steer the group to truth rather than dictate terms or sit in judgment.

2. Look for opinions, not answers. Ask what the person thinks or feels.

3. Foster an environment of open discussion. The participants will feel like it is their group and will be more likely to own what they discover and learn.

4. Pray for each person before, during, and after each group time. Prayer is your most important task.

5. Communicate clearly in what ways you need your helpers to assist.

The Small-Group Helpers

Serve as part of the Ministry Team and report to the Small-Group Leader.

The key responsibility of the Small-Group Helpers is to assist the Small-Group Leaders create a welcoming atmosphere where guests feel free to ask honest questions about the Christian faith.

Qualifications

A growing Christian or seeking non-Christian; is good with people; sensitive; understands from where nonchurchgoers are coming; nonjudgmental; and has a servant's heart.

Specific Responsibilities

1. Attend all training sessions, the opening Alpha Dinner, all weekly administrative/prayer meetings, each of 10 weekly Alpha sessions, the weekend away, any follow-up meetings, and the Celebration Dinner.

2. Read *Questions of Life* and *Searching Issues* (both by Nicky Gumbel) prior to the beginning of Alpha to become familiar with the course content and objections to the Christian faith which may come up during the course.

3. Prepare for each small-group time by reviewing the material and praying for the speaker, the other leaders and helpers, and each group member.

4. Be familiar with the material in chapter 5 of Telling Others and pages 18–44 of *The Alpha Course Leader's Guide*. If at all possible do not have the Leader's Guide in plain view during group time, especially during the early sessions. You want group members to discuss freely and not to feel you are following a script.

5. Help the discussion stay on course by asking questions.

6. Pray for each person before, during, and after every group time. Prayer is your most important task.

7. Assist your leaders in any way you are asked.

8. Prepare for each worship time by praying for the speaker, the Alpha Worship Leader, other Worship and Ministry Team Members, the guests, and yourself. Ask the Holy Spirit to reveal any area of your life where you need forgiveness and to fill you.

9. During the ministry times, pray for those who respond and indicate they would like prayer. Ministry times follow Talks 8 and 12. Remember the guidelines to pray in teams with a designated leader and to pray for members of your same sex.

10. If needed during the first three weeks, serve as a Greeter or Runner. See pages 55-56 for job descriptions.

The Greeters

Serve as members of the Alpha Team and report to the Small-Group Coordinator.

The Greeters are very important because they are among the first people the guests will meet. Their key responsibility is to make people feel welcome and glad they have come to Alpha.

Qualifications

Friendly (without being effusive); helpful; easygoing; good at remembering names and faces; reliable; nice outward appearance; and have a servant's heart.

Specific Responsibilities

1. Be familiar with each small group and that group's leaders, helpers, and members.
2. Know the location of each small group.
3. Inform each person of his or her small-group leader and location.
4. Assign guests who have not preregistered to an appropriate small group.
5. Introduce guests to a Runner who will take them to their small groups.

The Runners

Serve as members of the Alpha Team and report to the Small-Group Coordinator.

Since Runners are among the first people the guests meet, they are very important. Their main responsibility is to help people who are unfamiliar with the church and Alpha feel comfortable.

Qualifications

Friendly (without being effusive); helpful; good at remembering names and faces; reliable; nice outward appearance; and have a servant's heart.

Specific Responsibilities

1. Be familiar with each small group and that group's leaders, helpers, and members.
2. Display name tags for all team members and guests alphabetically and distribute them as people arrive.
3. Greet each guest as he or she is introduced by a Greeter and get that person to the correct small group.
4. Make name tags for guests who have not preregistered.
5. Return to the main door as quickly as possible after showing a guest to his or her group.

The Task Force Coordinator

Serves as a member of the Alpha Team and reports to the Director.

The key responsibility of this person is to select and train the Alpha Task Force—a team of people who provide practical services for the Alpha Course involving everything from helping with parking cars to cleanup.

Qualifications

A mature or growing Christian; experienced in overseeing and delegating responsibility to others; organized; able to train others; understands that the heart of Alpha is to provide a safe and comfortable environment where nonchurchgoers feel welcome; has good interpersonal skills; sensitive; gifted in areas of administration and help; and has a servant's heart.

Specific Responsibilities

1. Under the direction of the Church Leader and Director select and oversee the Task Force— a team of people who are responsible for logistics for the 10 weekly sessions, the Alpha Dinner (whether it is the first one before the first course begins or one after a course ends), and, in some cases, the Weekend Away. The size of the Task Force will vary depending on the number of people in attendance. Larger courses may want to appoint a person as the Alpha Dinner Coordinator (a separate job description is included). For smaller courses, the Task Force Coordinator can assume this responsibility.

2. Plan for all aspects of the weekly dinners including the menu, arrangement of tables, serving and eating dishes, cups and silverware, logistics of serving, cleanup, and evaluation.

3. Model spiritual leadership by being available to Task Force Members, praying for them regularly, and consistently affirming them.

4. Provide pastoral care as needed.

5. Attend all training sessions, the opening Alpha Dinner, all weekly administrative/prayer meetings, each of 10 weekly Alpha sessions, the Weekend Away, any follow-up meetings, and the Celebration Dinner.

6. Oversee the setup and location for each small group, assuring adequate lighting, temperature control, and seating. Make sure there are enough copies of a modern translation of the Bible, such as the New International Version, for each Small-Group Leader, Helper, and member to use during group time.

7. Emphasize to all Task Force Members the importance of commitment to the course. Remind them that they want to try for a standard of "100-percent excellence."

8. Lead (or delegate leadership for) a prayer time with the Task Force Members during the small-group meeting time.

9. Perform all the above functions as needed at the Weekend Away under the direction of the Weekend Away Coordinator. If the weekend is held at a full-service conference center, the Task Force will simply attend. It becomes their chance to relax and worship.

The Alpha Dinner Coordinator

Serves as a member of the Task Force and reports to the Task Force Coordinator.

The key responsibility of this person is to assure that enough quality food is prepared and available for the opening Alpha Dinner, each weekly dinner, and the Celebration Dinner at the end of the course.

Qualifications

A growing Christian; organized; is good with people; "full of the Spirit and wisdom" (Acts 6:4); has gifts in the areas of helps and administration; and has a servant's heart.

Specific Responsibilities

If the weekly meals are not catered:

1. In conjunction with the Task Force Coordinator, plan a menu for each weekly dinner. These dinners should be simple yet appetizing. Suggestions include pasta dishes (spaghetti, lasagna, mostaccioli, etc.), sloppy joe's or barbecues, chili con carne, one-dish casseroles, and pizza. Always have a vegetarian alternative. In addition to the main dish serve a vegetable or gelatin salad, bread or rolls, and a simple dessert.

2. Based on the size of the course, determine who will cook. With groups of 12-15, the leaders and helpers can take turns. For courses with up to about 10 groups (or 120 people), the small groups can take turns with the cooking. Once the attendance goes over 120-150 it works best to have a caterer. Try to keep the cost of the dinner to $3.00 to $5.00 per person.

If the weekly meals are catered:

1. In conjunction with the Treasurer and the caterer, determine the weekly menu to provide a variety of inexpensive meals. Check with fast food and other local restaurants as many offer catering. Try to keep the weekly cost below $7.00 per person.

2. Agree with the caterer on the number of servings needed. This may vary for the first few weekly dinners depending on how many guests continue coming.

Opening Alpha Dinner, closing Celebration Dinner

1. Select a menu that is similar to, but a little nicer than, the weekly dinners. Think in terms of what could be served for company rather than for family. If possible, cater this meal.

2. Communicate the actual cost to the Task Force Coordinator who will make sure all Small-Group Leaders tell the members of their groups. Group members pay for their own meals and their guests.

Weekend away

1. In conjunction with the Weekend Away Coordinator, determine what meals or snacks, if any, will be brought or prepared by the church.

2. Oversee the purchase and preparation of any food brought in for the weekend.

Task Force Members

Serve as members of the Task Force and report to the Task Force Coordinator.

The Task Force is to provide practical services for all aspects of the Alpha Course.

Qualifications

A growing Christian; is good with people; moving toward being "full of the Spirit and wisdom" (Acts 6:4); has beginning of gifts in the areas of helps and mercy; and has a servant's heart.

Specific Responsibilities

1. Help with parking cars—an important job. Remember that at the beginning of the course, those parking cars are the first people the guests will meet. Make sure to wear a smile and your name tag all the time to help guests feel welcome and get acquainted quickly.

2. Help serve the meal (unless done by the caterer) and make sure the guests have everything they need.

3. Set up all tables needed for the serving of dinner and coffee and all chairs for the small groups. Ensure that each small group is identified with a sign naming the group leaders and that each group has enough chairs, Bibles, and *Alpha Course Manuals.*

4. Place a pile of Bibles under one of the chairs in each small group. In this way the guests are not put off by seeing a Bible on every chair.

5. Prepare coffee, water for tea, and anything else needed for the coffee break.

6. If there is a book table with Alpha resources and related recommended books, help staff this table as needed.

7. Clean up tables, the serving area, and kitchen after the weekly dinners and Celebration Dinner.

8. Be willing to help in any way needed or as requested by the Task Force Coordinator.

The Book Table Coordinator

Serves as a member of the Alpha Team and reports to the Task Force Coordinator.

The key responsibility of this person is to order and maintain a stock of Alpha resources and related reading.

Qualifications

A mature or growing Christian; experienced in overseeing and delegating responsibility to others; organized; has good interpersonal skills; gifted in areas of administration and help; and has a servant's heart.

Specific Responsibilities

1. With the Alpha Director, determine quantity of all course materials (*The Alpha Course Manual* and *Leader's Guide, Why Jesus?* or *Why Christmas? Questions of Life, The Alpha Course Videos* or *DVDs, Searching Issues, How to Run the Alpha Course,* etc.) and related reading (see complete listing 91-94).

2. Order and maintain an adequate quantity of Alpha resources and related reading. (See page 94 for ordering information.)

The Treasurer

Serves as a member of the Alpha Team and reports to the Director.

This person is responsible for handling all budgets and finances related to the Alpha Course.

Qualifications

Experienced accountant or treasurer; reliable; honest; prompt; and has a servant's heart.

Specific Responsibilities

1. Prepare a budget for all aspects of the Alpha ministry including Alpha resources, cost of all meals and related expenses (flowers for Celebration Dinner, copy of *Why Jesus?* or *Why Christmas?* for each guest, caterer, etc.). See pages 31-32 for more information.

2. Meet with church treasurer/business manager to learn about church policies and procedures pertaining to the handling of funds.

3. In conjunction with the Alpha Dinner Coordinator, determine the cost of each weekly dinner. Collect money each week by placing baskets on each serving table.

4. Issue payment to the outside caterer or reimburse the Alpha Dinner Coordinator or whoever paid for the dinner supplies.

5. In conjunction with the Alpha Dinner Coordinator and the caterer, determine the per person cost for the Celebration Dinner and make this amount known to all Alpha Course participants by Week 8. People will pay for their own meal as well as the meals of any guests. All payments should be collected prior to the actual night of the dinner.

6. In conjunction with the Weekend Away Coordinator determine the per person cost of the Weekend Away. Publicize and collect funds at the time of registration.

7. Assist as needed in raising scholarships for those needing help to attend the event. This may be done with a collection on Sunday morning of the Weekend Away.

8. Arrange for a lockbox, if needed, at the weekend site to secure funds received on-site.

9. Develop a system of accountability for all income and expense associated with Alpha. (How is cash handled? Do checks need two signatures? How is registration income for the weekly dinner and Weekend Away accounted for? What safeguards are in place to insure integrity with all funds?)

10. Check on insurance coverage. Does your church have a policy that already covers any church-sponsored events? What insurance coverage is required by the Weekend Away facility, if any? Make sure the Weekend Away is adequately covered.

11. At the end of each Weekend Away and each Alpha Course, produce an income and expense report for the Alpha Director and church treasurer.

The Worship Leader

Serves as a member of the Alpha Team and reports to the Director.

This person oversees all aspects of worship times during the weekly Alpha sessions and the weekend away.

Qualifications

Competent musician and song leader; responsible; has understanding of philosophy of worship during Alpha; is versatile with music that appeals both to unchurched and growing Christian; has positive, teachable attitude; demonstrates mature Christian character; and has a servant's heart.

Specific Responsibilities

1. In conjunction with the Director, select songs for each worship time during Alpha including weekly sessions and the Weekend Away. Plan to use a mixture of old and new songs, beginning with a familiar hymn the first night and moving toward more modern songs. Change gradually from singing about God to singing directly to God.

2. Select a team of musicians whose lives well represent the Christian faith.

3. In conjunction with the Director, arrange for all sound equipment needed for the worship times and presentation and taping of the talks (if given live).

4. Arrange for songbooks or overheads with the words to all songs to be used during the weekly sessions and Weekend Away. Make sure use of all music and words of songs comply with copyright laws. If your church is a member of CCLI, please be sure to report this copying activity on your CCLI survey.

5. If the talks are presented via videotape, make arrangements for the video player and enough monitors (or a screen large enough) that everyone present will be able to view it easily.

6. If the talks are presented live, make sure that the microphone is in place and working properly, there is a podium or music stand for the speaker to place notes, and water is available for the speaker.

7. Attend all training sessions, the opening Alpha Dinner, all weekly administrative/prayer meetings, each of 10 weekly Alpha sessions, the Weekend Away, any follow-up meetings, and the Celebration Dinner.

The Weekend Away Coordinator

Serves as a member of the Alpha Team and reports to the Director.

The key responsibility of this person is to plan and oversee the Weekend Away by selecting and directing a team of workers who will facilitate all the practical aspects of the weekend.

Qualifications

A mature or growing Christian; experienced in overseeing and delegating responsibility to others; organized; able to train others; understands that the heart of Alpha is to provide a safe and comfortable environment where nonchurchgoers feel welcome; has good interpersonal skills; sensitive; gifted in areas of administration and help; and has a servant's heart.

Specific Responsibilities

1. Select and oversee people to organize the following aspects of the Weekend Away:
   - One-on-one informal counseling
   - Saturday evening entertainment
   - Sports and other free-time activities on Saturday afternoon
   - Child care, if you decide to have children come with their parents
   - Sunday morning Communion

2. Select and confirm a location for the weekend away within a one- or two-hour drive. During site selection ask the following questions:[1]
   - Can you handle a group of _____ (numbers) people on _____ (dates)? What is the maximum and minimum number of registrants your facility can accommodate?
   - What room accommodations are available? Can you provide sleeping rooms for the number of people expected? Are bathrooms private?
   - What is the size of your largest meeting room? What is the cost?
   - What food services can you provide and at what cost? (Obtain prices for snacks and meals; find out if the gratuity is included.) May we bring our own food, beverages, and/or snacks?
   - What meeting room equipment is provided (sound system, podium, overhead projector, etc.)? Will using this equipment cost extra? May we bring our own equipment?
   - What recreational facilities do you have? When are they open?

3. Obtain an agreement in writing from the facility specifying everything you discussed— menu, all costs for rooms and food, tips, meeting rooms, payment due dates and method, room types and prices, food or equipment you may bring, etc. Keep a copy on file at the church and carry a copy with you to the facility.

4. Obtain a map of how to get to the facility and a diagram of the facility. Duplicate and distribute this information to all attending.

5. Two or three weeks before the weekend, distribute a copy of the "Alpha Weekend Sign-Up Form" to each Small-Group Leader. A reproducible copy of this form is on page 87.

The Weekend Away Coordinator (cont.)

This form serves two purposes:

- To obtain information from those who will attend regarding special diets, need for rides, requests to room together, etc.
- To provide information to those planning to attend regarding cost and location.

Also provide a copy of the weekend schedule, map to the facility, and list of what to bring for each small-group member.

6. Check with the responsible person that the following items are available at the site:

- Task Force Leader—Books from the recommended reading list; supplies for Sunday morning Communion and for snacks and meals as planned.
- Worship Leader— Any audio/video equipment needed; songbooks or overhead transparencies.
- Treasurer—Cash box; checks to pay for all expenses; calculator; baskets for Sunday morning offering (which will be used to offset any amount individuals cannot afford); and all registration information including how much each person has paid.
- Alpha Dinner Coordinator—Food and beverage for any snacks or meals prepared and brought in by the church.

7. Make room assignments based on information obtained on the Weekend Sign-Up Form. Have this information available as people arrive.

[1]This information has been adapted from *Creative Weekends,* compiled by Paul Petersen (Colorado Springs: David C. Cook Publishing Co., 1995), p. 234. Used with permission.

The Weekend Entertainment Coordinator

Serves as part of the Alpha Team and reports to the Weekend Away Coordinator.

This person is responsible for organizing and directing the Saturday evening entertainment during the Weekend Away.

Qualifications

A mature or growing Christian; experienced in overseeing others; organized; has a good sense of humor; works well with people; has a servant's heart.

Specific Responsibilities

1. Publicize the Saturday entertainment night beginning one or two weeks prior to the Weekend Away.

2. Set up times for individuals or groups to register their "acts." Obtain the following information for each potential act: names, phone numbers, the type of act, content or script, and approximate length.

3. Screen all entertainment, making sure it is wholesome and inoffensive to Christians and non-Christians alike. The intent of this evening is good, clean fun. Therefore, avoid anything "religious" and don't expect professional quality. Everything from skits, stand-up comedy, and singing, to "magic," monologues, and dramatic readings work well.

4. Develop a sequence for the Saturday night program which offers variety. That is, you do not want three soloists in a row!

5. Serve as emcee for the talent review.

6. Lead the audience in affirming each person who is brave enough to participate in the entertainment.

Planning Timeline

Director_____ Phone_____ E-mail _____

Date of Alpha Dinner_____ Date Course Starts _____

Thank you for agreeing to serve on the Alpha Team or Alpha Task Force. Please check over this timeline for the tasks assigned to you. Adapt as needed. Supplement this timeline with your specific job description. Highlight your tasks and due date each time they appear. Mark your calendar accordingly.

7 TO 9 MONTHS IN ADVANCE
DATE_____ **Church Leader**

☐ Determine with the church staff and Alpha Team leaders whether the talks will be presented live or via videotape. If any will be presented live, select the speaker(s) and assign the talks.

☐ Attend an Alpha Conference with the Director and as many of your Alpha Team leaders and church staff as possible.

Director

☐ Attend an Alpha Conference with as many of your Alpha Team leaders and church staff as possible.

☐ With the Church Leader set the exact dates for the opening Alpha Dinner, the Alpha Course, the weekend away, and the closing Celebration Dinner. Reserve all church facilities that will be needed for each event.

☐ Based on the anticipated size of the course, select a site for the Alpha Dinner and weekly meetings.

☐ With the Church Leader, select people to serve in the following roles: Small-Group Coordinator, Task Force Coordinator, Treasurer, Worship Leader, and Weekend Away Coordinator. Make sure each leader on the Alpha Team understands his or her responsibilities. Distribute copies of appropriate job descriptions to all Alpha Team members.

6 MONTHS IN ADVANCE
DATE_____ **Director**

☐ Hold the first Alpha Team meeting. Review this timeline, adjust as needed, and fill in due dates. Distribute a copy to each Alpha Team member.

☐ Seek God's guidance for the selection of Small-Group Leaders and Helpers.

Task Force Coordinator

☐ Based on the anticipated size of the course, determine whether you will need an Alpha Dinner Coordinator. Recruit this person if needed.

☐ In conjunction with the Treasurer, begin developing a budget for the Alpha Dinner (to be held before the beginning of your first Alpha Course), weekly Alpha sessions, Celebration Dinner (following each Alpha Course), and Weekend Away.

☐ Seek God's guidance in the selection of the Alpha Dinner Coordinator and other Task Force Members.

Planning Timeline

☐ Begin developing a budget for the Alpha Course as well as for the Weekend Away.

☐ Meet with the church treasurer/business manager to learn about church policies pertaining to handling funds. Throughout the Alpha ministry implement these policies.

Weekend Away Coordinator

☐ With the Alpha Team's input, carefully choose one or two facilities as potential locations for the Weekend Away. Contact and evaluate these facilities based on the anticipated weekend attendance and make a selection as soon as possible.

☐ Obtain a written agreement from the facility specifying everything you discussed.

☐ In conjunction with the Treasurer, develop a budget for the Weekend Away.

5 MONTHS IN ADVANCE
DATE_____

Director

☐ Meet with the Alpha Team to pray and discuss progress. Report progress to the Church Leader.

4 MONTHS IN ADVANCE
DATE_____

Director

☐ Meet with the Alpha Team to pray and discuss progress. Report progress to the Church Leader.

3 MONTHS IN ADVANCE
DATE_____

Director

☐ Meet with the Alpha Team to pray and discuss progress. Report progress to the Church Leader.

☐ Order (or make sure the Book Table Coordinator has ordered) an adequate supply of Alpha resources and any related reading. Make sure each member of the Alpha Team and Task Force has a copy of *Questions of Life*. All coordinators and Small-Group Leaders and Helpers should also read *How to Run the Alpha Course: The Director's Handbook, Telling Others,* and *Searching Issues* prior to the start of the course. Leaders and Helpers need copies of the *Alpha Course Manual* and *Leader's Guide*. Order enough copies of *Why Jesus?* (or *Why Christmas?* depending on the season) to distribute on the second Alpha Sunday and at the Alpha Dinner.

Small-Group Coordinator

☐ With the Church Leader and Director, select the Small-Group Leaders and Helpers. Determine which helpers will also serve on the Ministry Team.

☐ Send letter of invitation to serve (signed by the Church Leader) to all Small-Group Leaders and Helpers.

Planning Timeline

Task Force Coordinator

☐ Based on the size of your course, determine the size of the Task Force and select each member. Send letter of invitation to serve (signed by the Church Leader) to each Task Force Member.

☐ Meet with your team to assign jobs.

Treasurer

☐ Develop a system of accounting for all income and expenses for the course.

☐ Check on insurance coverage and make arrangements for coverage for all aspects of the course as needed.

Worship Leader

☐ Select a team of musicians and singers. Set a practice schedule to assure quality music each week.

☐ Arrange for all audio/video equipment for the weekly sessions and weekend.

2 MONTHS IN ADVANCE
DATE_____   **Director**

☐ Meet with the Alpha Team to discuss progress and pray for each team member and expected guest. Report progress to the Church Leader.

Small-Group Leaders/Helpers (Ministry Team)

☐ Read *Questions of Life* and *Searching Issues* and review this book, *How to Run the Alpha Course: The Director's Handbook.*

☐ Become familiar with the philosophy of pastoral care and ministry as explained in various Alpha resources. (See job description.)

4 WEEKS IN ADVANCE
DATE_____   **Director**

☐ Meet with the Alpha Team to discuss progress and pray for each team member and expected guest. Report progress to the Church Leader.

☐ Either customize the Alpha brochure (see pages 39-40 and 79 for more information) or create and print your own brochure. Write a brief letter of invitation which includes the dates, times, location, and phone number of Alpha and the names of all the talks. (See page 85 for a sample letter.)

Task Force Coordinator or Alpha Dinner Coordinator

☐ Plan the weekly dinner menus.

☐ Make arrangements with the caterer or make cooking assignments.

Treasurer

☐ Finalize budget for all aspects of Alpha including each meal, the Weekend Away, all flowers, resources, and other incidentals.

Planning Timeline

Worship Leader

☐ Select songs for each weekly session and the Weekend Away. As necessary, seek permission to print and display the words.

☐ Begin weekly practices to ensure quality music and singing at all Alpha events.

3 WEEKS IN ADVANCE

DATE_____

Director

☐ Meet with the Alpha Team to discuss progress and pray for each team member and expected guest. Report to Church Leader.

☐ Insert a flyer about Alpha in all worship bulletins. Have Alpha Registration brochures available at all services.

Weekend Away Coordinator

☐ Select people to organize and implement these aspects of the Weekend Away: informal counseling, Saturday evening entertainment, free-time activities, child care, and the Sunday morning communion service.

2 WEEKS IN ADVANCE

DATE_____

Church Leader

☐ Meet with the Alpha Team to discuss progress and pray for each team member and expected guest.

☐ Conduct the first of three training sessions for the Small-Group Leaders and Helpers. The topic will be "Leading Small Groups".

Director

☐ Meet with the Alpha Team to discuss progress and pray for each team member and expected guest.

☐ Insert a flyer about Alpha in all worship bulletins. Have Alpha Registration brochures available at all services.

☐ Hold the first "Alpha Sunday". Share a true story of a life changed through attending Alpha. For your first Alpha, select one from *Alpha News* or *The God Who Changes Lives* by Mark Elsdon-Dew. For subsequent courses, plan on using impromptu interviews as explained on page 31. Encourage everyone to invite friends and family to church next Sunday.

Small-Group Coordinator

☐ With the Director, assign all leaders, helpers, and guests to small groups. Encourage the leaders and helpers to begin praying for their group members.

Small-Group Leaders/Helpers

☐ Attend the first of three training sessions. The topic will be "Leading Small Groups".

☐ Be familiar with the content of chapter 5 of *Telling Others* and pages 18-44 of the *Alpha Course Leader's Guide*.

Worship Leader

☐ Arrange for songbooks or overheads for all songs to be used throughout Alpha.

Planning Timeline

1 WEEK IN ADVANCE
DATE_____   **Church Leader**

☐ Hold the second of three training sessions. The topic will be "Pastoral Care".

Director

☐ Insert a flyer about Alpha in all worship bulletins. Have Alpha registration brochures available at all services.

☐ Hold the second Alpha Sunday. Include a short testimony of the impact of Alpha. Distribute brochures and complimentary copies of *Why Jesus?* (or *Why Christmas?* depending on the season) to anyone interested. The pastor's message should be evangelistic. Close the service with an invitation to attend Alpha.

Small-Group Leaders/Helpers & (Ministry Team) and Task Force

☐ Attend the second of three training sessions. The topic will be "Pastoral Care".

Task Force Coordinator or Alpha Dinner Coordinator

☐ If using a caterer, make final arrange-ments for the number of expected guests.

ALPHA DINNER
DATE_____   **Church Leader**

☐ Present the talk "Christianity: Boring, Untrue, and Irrelevant?" or introduce the recorded talk.

Director

☐ Serve as the emcee. Keep the tone relaxed and friendly. Use of humor will help the guests relax.

Entire Alpha Team

☐ Arrive early with a servant's attitude. Pray for all aspects of the evening.

Alpha Dinner Coordinator

☐ Oversee all aspects of the preparation of the meal.

Task Force Coordinator

☐ Oversee all aspects of the serving and cleanup of the meal.

Task Force Members

☐ Welcome and serve the guests with natural friendliness.
☐ Set the tables and have copies of *Why Jesus?* (or *Why Christmas?*) at guests' tables or at the exit doors.
☐ Make sure the room temperature is comfortable and the lighting is good.
☐ Complete all tasks as directed by the Coordinator.

Planning Timeline

Worship Leader

☐ Make sure all audiovisual equipment is in place before guests arrive. If using video, set up the video player and monitor(s). For live speakers, make sure the microphone and podium are in place for the speaker.

WEEK 1 OF ALPHA *(and all other sessions during Alpha)*
DATE _____
Church Leader

☐ Present the scheduled talk or introduce the recorded talk. See page 28 for sequence of talks.
☐ During the talks and ministry times, pray for each Ministry Team Member, and all who respond during the ministry times.

Director

☐ Conduct the administration and prayer meeting prior to each dinner.

Treasurer

☐ Place baskets on each serving table and collect money to cover the weekly dinners.
☐ Pay the outside caterer or reimburse those in the church who purchased the dinner supplies.

All Alpha Team Members

☐ Arrive in time for the weekly administration and prayer meeting.

Task Force Coordinator

☐ Oversee all practical aspects of the course.
☐ Lead (or delegate the leadership of) a prayer time with the Task Force Members while the small groups are meeting.

Task Force

☐ Set up chairs and display a sign for each small group. Make sure there are enough Bibles and Alpha Course manuals for each group.
☐ Help park cars, greet guests, and direct them to their small groups. Make sure each guest and Alpha Team Member has a name tag.
☐ Serve food and beverages during the dinner and coffee break. Make sure the eating and meeting area(s) are spotless at the end of each session.
☐ Help with book sales at the book table.

Small-Group Leaders/Helpers (Ministry Team)

☐ Pray for the speaker, all other Small-Group Leaders and Helpers, the guests, and all aspects of Alpha.

Worship Leader

☐ Make sure all audiovisual equipment is in place before guests arrive. If using video, set up the video player and monitor(s). For live speakers, make sure the microphone and podium are in place after the worship time.

Planning Timeline

WEEK 2 OF ALPHA

DATE_____ **Treasurer**

❑ With the Weekend Away Coordinator, determine the cost per person for the weekend away. Arrange for a lockbox at the weekend.

Weekend Away Coordinator

❑ Distribute copies of the Alpha Weekend Sign-up Form to Small-Group Leaders. Include the weekend schedule, map to the facility, and list of what to bring.

WEEK 3 OF ALPHA

DATE_____ **Weekend Entertainment Coordinator**

❑ Begin publicizing the Saturday entertainment by providing sign-up sheets for individual or group "acts". Be sensitive to the feelings of the potential participants as you screen the "acts".

WEEK 4 OF ALPHA

DATE_____ **Weekend Away Coordinator**

❑ Finalize the count for the weekend. Make room assignments; have copies available at the registration table there.

❑ Meet with your team of volunteers to assure all aspects of the weekend are covered as listed in your job description.

WEEK 5 OF ALPHA

DATE_____ **Task Force Coordinator or Alpha Dinner Coordinator**

❑ Oversee the purchase and preparation of any food the church will provide at the weekend away.

Weekend Entertainment Coordinator

❑ Develop the order of entertainment and communicate this to each participant.

WEEK 6 OF ALPHA

DATE_____ **Church Leader**

❑ Present the talk "How Does God Guide Us?" or introduce the recorded talk.

WEEKEND AWAY

DATE_____

❑ See job descriptions for specific information.

Planning Timeline

WEEK 7 OF ALPHA

DATE_____
                                                                        Director

☐ Begin promoting the Celebration Dinner and distribute invitations for the small-group members to use for their friends and families.

Small-Group Leaders

☐ During the small-group time allow time for personal sharing about the weekend away.

WEEK 8 OF ALPHA

DATE_____   **Task Force Coordinator or Alpha Dinner Coordinator**

☐ Select a menu for the Celebration Dinner. Communicate the cost per dinner to the Task Force Coordinator who will give this information to the Small-Group Leaders.

Small-Group Leaders

☐ Distribute copies of the Celebration Dinner invitation to group members.

WEEK 9 OF ALPHA

DATE_____
                                                                    Church Leader

☐ Oversee the Ministry Team during the ministry time.

Small-Group Leaders/Helpers (Ministry Team)

☐ Be available to pray for those who respond during the ministry time following the guidelines in chapter 7 of *Telling Others* and Session 3 of the *Alpha Leader's Training Videos* or *DVDs*.

WEEK 10 OF ALPHA

DATE_____
                                                                        Treasurer

☐ Finalize the count for the Celebration Dinner. Collect payment for the Celebration Dinner for each person and his or her guests.

CELEBRATION DINNER

DATE_____
                                                                    Church Leader

☐ Present the talk "Christianity: Boring, Untrue, and Irrelevant?" or introduce the recorded talk.

Director

☐ Serve as the emcee. Keep the tone relaxed and friendly. Use of humor will help the guests relax.

Entire Alpha Team

☐ Arrive early with a servant's attitude. Pray for all aspects of the evening.

Planning Timeline

Alpha Dinner Coordinator

☐ Oversee all aspects of the preparation of the meal.

Task Force Coordinator

☐ Oversee all aspects of the serving and cleanup of the meal.

Task Force Members

☐ Welcome and serve the guests with natural friendliness.
☐ Set the tables and have copies of *Why Jesus?* (or *Why Christmas?*) available for guests at their tables or at the exits.
☐ Make sure the room temperature is comfortable and the lighting is good.
☐ Complete all tasks as directed by the Coordinator.

Worship Leader

☐ Make sure all audiovisual equipment is in place before guests arrive. If using video, set up the video player and monitor(s). For live speakers, make sure the microphone and podium are in place for the speaker.

1 WEEK AFTER ALPHA COURSE ENDS
DATE_____   **Director**

☐ Meet with the Alpha Team to go over the completed Alpha Questionnaires, evaluate all aspects of the course, affirm and thank each person, and determine necessary changes for the next course. Make adjustments in the Alpha Team as needed to have all positions filled for the next course.

Small-Group Leaders

☐ Complete and turn in an Alpha Follow-up Form (see page 89 for a reproducible form).

Treasurer

☐ Prepare and submit an income and expense report for all Alpha expenses.

Schedules

SCHEDULE FOR EVENING ALPHA

6:15 or 6:30 P.M.	Leaders and helpers meet to pray
7:00 P.M.	Dinner is served
7:40 P.M.	Welcome
7:50 P.M.	Songs of worship
8:00 P.M..	Talk
8:45 P.M.	Coffee
9:00 P.M.	Small groups
9:45 P.M.	End

SCHEDULE FOR DAYTIME ALPHA

10:00 A.M.	Child care opens
10:20 A.M.	Welcome & coffee Worship
10:30 A.M.	Talk
11:15 A.M.	Additional short coffee break
11:20 A.M.	Small groups
12:00 P.M	Finish

SCHEDULE FOR ALL-DAY SATURDAY ONLY

9:15 a.m.	Registration and coffee
9:30 a.m.	Worship
10:00 a.m.	Talk 1 - Combine "Who Is the Holy Spirit?"and "What Does the Holy Spirit Do? *(on Video 3, #8 and #9)*
10:45 a.m.	Small groups and session
11:30 a.m.	Talk 2 - "How Can I Be Filled with the Holy Spirit? *(on Video 4, #10)*
1:30p.m.	Lunch
2:15 p.m.	Worship
2:30 p.m.	Worship Talk 3 - "How Can I Make the Most of the Rest of My Life?" *(on Video 5, #15)* followed by communion and ministry
4:30 p.m.	Coffee break
5:00 p.m.	Finish

Schedules

SCHEDULE FOR WEEKEND AWAY

Full Weekend Schedule

Friday

6:30 P.M. onward	Arrive
8:00 P.M.	Dinner
9:45 P.M.	Worship and a brief introduction to the weekend

Saturday

8:30 A.M.	Breakfast
9:00 A.M.	Leader's meeting
9:30 A.M.	Worship
	Talk 1 - "Who Is the Holy Spirit?"
10:45 A.M.	Coffee
11:15 A.M.	Talk 2 - "What Does the Holy Spirit Do?"
12:00 P.M.	Small group discussion
1:00 P.M.	Lunch
Free Afternoon	Optional sports and activities will be offered
4:15 P.M.	Optional refreshments
5:00 P.M.	Worship
	Talk 3 - "How Can I Be filled with the Spirit?"
7:00 P.M.	Dinner
8:30 P.M.	Talent Show *(you are invited to participate)*

Sunday

9:00 A.M.	Breakfast
9:20 A.M.	Leader's meeting
9:45 A.M.	Small group discussion
10:30 A.M.	Worship
	Talk 4 - "How Can I Make the Most of the Rest of My Life?"
	Communion
1:00 P.M.	Lunch

Remember to bring:

- Bible, *Alpha Course Manual,* pen or pencil, and notebook
- Personal toiletries
- Sports gear (tennis racket, Frisbee, swimsuit, etc.)
- Props, costumes, music, or anything needed for the Talent Show!

Promotion of Alpha

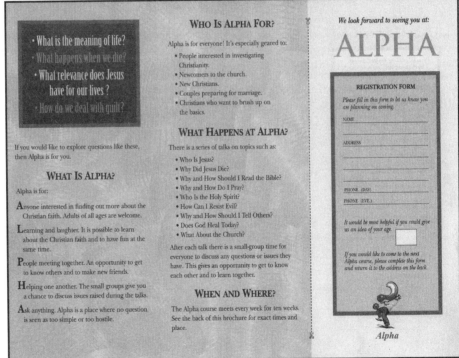

The Alpha Invitation Brochure (unfolded, front and back sides)
Note that you can customize the back panel to include the specific dates,
times, and location of your local Alpha Course.

Press Release

THE ALPHA COURSE

(Name of sponsoring group/church) will begin the Alpha Course on (date), at (time), at (place).

This ten-week practical introduction to the Christian faith offers answers to some key questions. Each weekly session begins with an informal dinner, followed by a large-group learning time, and ends with small-group discussion and interaction. Alpha began in London and is now held in thousands of churches around the world. Join the thousands who have found answers to their questions about life and God and how they relate.

To learn more about the course, call (number of Alpha Director) or come to the Alpha Dinner on (date), at (time), at (location). For reservations, call (church number) between (daily hours).

Bulletin Inserts

Coming soon . . .

The Alpha Course

A 10-Week Practical Introduction to the Christian Faith

Alpha

Anyone can come. Anyone interested in finding out more about the Christian faith is welcome.

Learning and laughter. Join others in a relaxed atmosphere.

Pasta (or other great food). Each weekly session begins with dinner.

Helping one another. Dinner is followed by large-group presentation and small-group discussion.

Ask anything. Here's your chance to ask your questions and express your opinions.

When:

Where:

For more information call:

Bulletin Inserts

PRESENTING

The Alpha Course

A 10-Week Practical Introduction to the Christian Faith

❖ Dinner   ❖ Small-group discussion
❖ Group teaching   ❖ Weekend away

A 10-week program for those who wonder:
   ❖ Christianity: Boring, Untrue, and Irrelevant?
   ❖ Who Is Jesus?
   ❖ Why Did Jesus Die?
   ❖ How Can I Be Sure of My Faith?
   ❖ Why and How Should I Read the Bible?
   ❖ Why and How Do I Pray?
   ❖ How Does God Guide Us?
   ❖ Who Is the Holy Spirit?
   ❖ How Can I Be Filled with the Spirit?
   ❖ What Does the Holy Spirit Do?
   ❖ How Can I Resist Evil?
   ❖ Why and How Should We Tell Others?
   ❖ Does God Heal Today?
   ❖ What About the Church?

Alpha Questionnaire

Name_____   Group _____

1. How did you hear about the Alpha Course? _____

_____

2. Why did you decide to attend Alpha? _____

_____

3. Did you attend the Alpha Dinner party?   ❐ yes   ❐ no

4. How many of the weekly sessions did you attend? _____

5. Did you attend the Weekend Away?   ❐ yes   ❐ no

6. Before you started the course, how would you have described yourself in terms of the Christian faith? _____

_____

7. Were you a Christian when you started the course?   ❐ yes   ❐ no

8. Were you a churchgoer when you started the course?   ❐ yes   ❐ no

9. How would you describe yourself now in terms of the Christian faith? _____

_____

If your answers to questions 6 and 9 are different, when and how did the change occur?

_____

10. In what ways, if any, did you benefit from the Alpha Course? _____

_____

11. What did you enjoy most about Alpha? _____

_____

12. In what ways could the course be improved?

    Talks _____

    Small Groups _____   anything else?

    Other _____

Sample Alpha Invitation Letter

Holy Trinity Brompton
Brompton Road, London SW7 1JA
Telephone: 0171 581 8255 Fax: 0171 589 3390

We would like to invite you to join us on the Alpha Course which begins Wednesday, January 19. Alpha is a short, practical introduction to the Christian faith. It includes an optional weekend away. This is a key part of the course, as well as being great fun, so please write the dates on your calendar now. Further details will be available later.

We will be leading the course with a team. Each evening begins with supper at 7:00 P.M., includes a talk, and ends with an opportunity to meet in small groups to discuss and study the Bible. All meetings will take place on Wednesday evenings at Holy Trinity Brompton.

Please return your complete registration form to the church office by January 6. We look forward to meeting you.

—Nicky and Pippa Gumbel

January 19	Who Is Jesus?
January 26	Why Did Jesus Die?
February 2	How Can I Be Sure of My Faith?
February 9	Why and How Should I Read the Bible?
February 16	Why and How Do I Pray?
February 23	How Does God Guide Us?
February 25-27	The Holy Spirit Weekend Away
March 1	How Can I Resist Evil?
March 8	Why and How Should We Tell Others?
March 15	Does God Heal Today?
March 22	What About the Church?
March 29	Alpha Dinner party (I)
April 5	Alpha Dinner party (II)

Alpha Weekend Sign-up Form

Group Number ____		Date ____				Notes
First Name	Last Name	Total Due	Check	Cash	Amt. Due	(Late arrivals, special diet, roommate requests, room in car, etc.)

Alpha Follow-up Form

Alpha Date _____ Group Number _____	First Name	Last Name	Completed the course? Yes or No	If no, why not?	Record name of small group (if any)	Alpha helper? Task force? Testimony?

Suggested Reading & Alpha Resources

RELATED READING

The following books are recommended to complement the Alpha Course. While the suggested books follow the course sequence, they can be read in any order.

Title	Author	Publishers	ISBN No.
Talk 1- Christianity: Boring, Untrue and Irrelevant?			
Why Jesus?	Nicky Gumbel	ANA	1-931808-090
Why Christmas?	Nicky Gumbel	ANA	1-931808-104
Talk 2 - Who Is Jesus?			
Questions of Life	Nicky Gumbel	Cook Communications	0-781452-619
Talk 3 - Why Did Jesus Die?			
Mere Christianity	C.S. Lewis	Touchstone	0-684823-780
Basic Christianity	John Stott	InterVarsity Press	0-877846-901
Orthodoxy	G.K. Chesterton	House of Stratus	0-755100-182
Talk 4 - How Can I Be Sure Of My Faith?			
Run Baby Run	Nicky Cruz	Logos & Assoc.	0-882706-306
The Cross & the Switchblade	David Wilkerson	Jove Publishing	0-515090-255
The Hiding Place	Corrie Ten Boom	Revell	0-800792-475
Talk 5 - Why And How Should I Read The Bible?			
Holy Bible	New International Version	Zondervan	0-310907-675
How to Read the Bible for All Its Worth	Gordon Fee & Douglas Stuart	Zondervan	0-310384-915
New Lion Handbook to the Bible		Lion	0-745938-701
30 Days	Nicky Gumbel	ANA	1-931808-112
Talk 6 - Why And How Do I Pray			
Too Busy Not to Pray	Bill Hybels	IVP	0-830819-711
How to Pray	Torrey	Moody Press	0-802437-095
Talk 7 - How Does God Guide Us?			
The Joy of Listening to God	Joyce Huggett	Hodder & Stoughton	0-340392-746
Talk 8 - Who is The Holy Spirit?			
Chasing the Dragon	Jackie Pullinger	IVP	0-877847-290

Title	Author	Publishers	ISBN No.
Talk 9 - What Does The Holy Spirit Do?			
The God Who Changes Lives Vol.1	Mark Elsdon-Dew (ed.)	ANA	1-931808-120
The God Who Changes Lives Vol.2	Mark Elsdon-Dew (ed.)	ANA	1-931808-139
The God Who Changes Lives Vol.3	Mark Elsdon-Dew (ed.)	Alpha International	1-902750-624
Talk 10 - How Can I Be Filled With The Spirit?			
Paul, the Spirit and the People of God	Gorden D.Fee	Hendrickson	1-565631-706
The Mystery of Pentecost	Raniero Cantalamessa	Vineyard Publishing	9-715048-48X
(Theological book for the advanced reader)			
Talk 11 - How Can I Resist Evil?			
The Screwtape Letters	C.S. Lewis	Simon & Schuster	0-684831-171
Talk 12 - Why And How Should We Tell Others?			
Searching Issues	Nicky Gumbel	Cook Communications	0-781452-597
The Case Against Christ	John Young	Hodder & Staughton	0-340524-626
The Heart of Revival	Nicky Gumbel	ANA	1-902750-357
Talk 13 - Does God Heal Today?			
Dancer Off Her Feet	Julie Sheldon	Hodder & Stoughton	0-340544-856
Talk 14 - What About The Church			
I Believe in the Church	David Watson	Hodder & Staughton	0–340745-541
Talk 15 - How Can I Make The Most Of The Rest Of My Life?			
Challenging Lifestyle	Nicky Gumbel	ANA	1-931808-163
Life in Christ	Raniero Cantalamessa	Vineyard Publishing	9-715048-48X
(Theological book for the advanced reader)			
Additional Resources			
Alpha Cookbook		ANA	1-931808-007
Maximizing the Potential of Your Alpha Course		ANA	1-931808-015

To obtain these resources visit your local Christian bookstore,
or call Alpha Resources at 1-800-36-ALPHA .

ALPHA RESOURCES

For additional information about Alpha resources, see pages 13-14 and 28-29.

This handbook is an Alpha resource. The Alpha Course is a practical introduction to the Christian faith developed by Holy Trinity Brompton Church in London, England. Alpha Courses are being run worldwide.

Resources needed for setting up the Alpha Course (training)
- *The Alpha Course Introductory Video* (15222)
- *How to Run the Alpha Course Videos,* set of 2 (65045)
- *Alpha Leader's Training DVD* (25603) OR • *Training Video* (25601) OR • *Tapes* (15248)
- *The Alpha Course Leader's Guide* (15388: one for each Small-Group Leader and Helper)
- *How to Run the Alpha Course: The Director's Handbook* (17160)
- *How to Run the Alpha Course: Telling Others* (16618)

Resources needed for running the Alpha Course
- *The Alpha Course DVDs* (15151) OR • *Videos* (15149)
- *The Alpha Course Manual* (15305: one for each guest, Small-Group Leader, and Helper)
- *The Alpha Course Leader's Guide* (15388: one for each Small-Group Leader and Helper)
- Invitation Brochures—several styles available (15446: pack of 50)
- *Why Jesus?* (20073) OR • *Why Christmas?* (20081)
- *Questions of Life* (15396)
- *Searching Issues* (15412)
- *Searching Issues Booklets:* Each booklet addresses one of the seven most-asked questions on Alpha.

ALPHA BOOKS

by Nicky Gumbel

- *Why Jesus?* (20073) A booklet recommended for all participants at the start of the Alpha Course.

- *Why Christmas?* (20081) The Christmas version of *Why Jesus?*

- *Questions of Life* The Alpha Course in book form. In fifteen compelling chapters the author points the way to an authentic Christianity which is exciting and relevant to today's world.

- *Searching Issues* The seven issues most often raised by participants of the Alpha Course: suffering, other religions, sex before marriage, the New Age, homosexuality, science and Christianity, and the Trinity.

- *A Life Worth Living* What happens after Alpha? Based on the Book of Philippians, this is an invaluable next step for those who have just completed the Alpha Course, and for anyone eager to put their faith on a firm biblical footing.

• *Challenging Lifestyle* An in-depth look at the Sermon on the Mount (Matthew 5–7). The author shows that Jesus' teaching flies in the face of modern lifestyle and presents us with a radical alternative.

• *How to Run the Alpha Course: The Director's Handbook* This book includes the principles and practicalities of setting up and running an Alpha Course. It also includes many reproducible resources for use with Alpha.

• *How to Run the Alpha Course: Telling Others* This book includes the principles and practicalities of setting up and running an Alpha Course.

• *The Heart of Revival* Ten studies on Isaiah 40-66, drawing out important truths for today. This course seeks to understand what revival might mean and how we can be part of it.

• *30 Days* Follow Nicky through 30 days of focused Bible reading and prayer to see how God's Word and His Spirit can change your life.

In North America, resources are published by Alpha North America.
To order any of the resources or books above, contact your local bookstore, or:

Alpha U.S.A.
74 Trinity Place
New York, NY 10006
Tel: 888.949.2574
Fax: 212.406.7521
e-mail: info@alphausa.org
www.alphausa.org

Alpha Canada
1620 W. 8th Ave, Suite 300
Vancouver, BC V6J 1V4
Tel: 800.743.0899
Fax: 604.224.6124
e-mail: office@alphacanada.org
www.alphacanada.org

To purchase resources in Canada:

Cook Communications Ministries
P.O. Box 98, 55 Woodslee Avenue
Paris, ONT N3L 3E5
Tel: 800.263.2664
Fax: 800.461.8575
e-mail: custserv@cook.ca
www.cook.ca

The Alpha Course

Time of Use	Talk Title	Questions of Life	Alpha Course Video or DVD	Alpha Course Manual	Alpha Course Leader's Guide Part II
Alpha Dinner	Christianity: Boring, Untrue, and Irrelevant?	Chapter 1	Talk 1	Chapter 1	—
Week 1	Who Is Jesus?	Chapter 2	Talk 2	Chapter 2	Chapter 1
Week 2	Why Did Jesus Die?	Chapter 3	Talk 3	Chapter 3	Chapter 2
Week 3	How Can I Be Sure of My Faith?	Chapter 4	Talk 4	Chapter 4	Chapter 3
Week 4	Why and How Should I Read the Bible?	Chapter 5	Talk 5	Chapter 5	Chapter 4
Week 5	Why and How Do I Pray?	Chapter 6	Talk 6	Chapter 6	Chapter 5
Week 6	How Does God Guide Us?	Chapter 7	Talk 7	Chapter 7	Chapter 6
Weekend Talk 1	Who Is the Holy Spirit?	Chapter 8	Talk 8	Chapter 8	Chapter 7
Weekend Talk 2	What Does the Holy Spirit Do?	Chapter 9	Talk 9	Chapter 9	Chapter 8
Weekend Talk 3	How Can I Be Filled with the Spirit?	Chapter 10	Talk 10	Chapter 10	Chapter 9
Weekend Talk 4	How Can I Make the Most of the Rest of My Life?	Chapter 15	Talk 15	Chapter 15	—
Week 7	How Can I Resist Evil?	Chapter 11	Talk 11	Chapter 11	Chapter 10
Week 8	Why and How Should We Tell Others?	Chapter 12	Talk 12	Chapter 12	Chapter 11
Week 9	Does God Heal Today?	Chapter 13	Talk 13	Chapter 13	Chapter 12
Week 10	What About the Church?	Chapter 14	Talk 14	Chapter 14	Chapter 13
Alpha Dinner	Christianity: Boring, Untrue, and Irrelevant?	Chapter 1	Talk 1	Chapter 1	—

Alpha Copyright Statement

The Directors of Alpha International write:

We have always desired to allow individuals who are running an Alpha International Course the flexibility to adapt where it was felt necessary to allow for locally felt needs and where there was the desire to retain the essential elements, nature, and identity of the course. Experience has shown though that this has been misunderstood and the resulting loss of integrity in some courses has given rise to considerable confusion. Now that Alpha International resources and publications are being used all around the world, we have reluctantly had to draw up a copyright statement more tightly in order to preserve confidence and quality control. We are sure you will understand.

1. With the exception of books published by Kingsway (in which the author is stated to hold the copyright), all Alpha International publications and materials including booklets, tapes, and graphics are copyright to Alpha International. Alpha International publications cover a wide range of ministries including The Alpha Course, The Marriage Course, An Introduction to Prayer Ministry, and Dynamic Prayer in the Local Church.

2. In no circumstances may any part of any Alpha International publication be reproduced or transmitted in any form or by any means, electronic or mechanical, including photocopying, recording, or any information storage or retrieval system without permission in writing from the copyright holder or that holder's agent.

3. Use of Alpha International publications is permitted only when in conjunction with the running or promotion of Alpha International courses. Resale, or the obtaining of payment in any other connection with any Alpha International publication is not permitted.

4. Alpha International asks that the name "Alpha" or names similar to it should not be used in connection with any other Christian course. This request is made in order to: avoid confusion caused by different courses having similar titles ensure the uniformity and integrity of the Alpha Course; and to maintain confidence in courses listed on the Alpha register.

5. Alpha International accepts that minor adaptations to Alpha International courses may occasionally be desirable. These should only concern the length of the talks or the number of sessions. In each case the essential character of the course must be retained.

If an Alpha International course is adapted the person responsible must: only use such a course in their own church or parish; not allow such a course to be used elsewhere; and not publish or promote such a course.

This statement supersedes all previous statements relating to copyright in any Alpha International publication.

Revised September 2002